CHRISTOPHER COLUMBUS

THE HERO

CHRISTOPHER COLUMBUS

THE HERO

DEFENDING COLUMBUS FROM MODERN DAY REVISIONISM

By *Rafael.*

ISBN-13:
978-1548738129

ISBN-10:
1548738123

To my wife Nina, to my children Sekel, Noa, and Logan.

Contents

Introduction

It is incredible how many Americans are willing, and happy to celebrate St. Patrick's Day, which has nothing to do with American history, than to celebrate Christopher Columbus, who discovered America and impacted world history like no other person, besides Jesus Christ. Ignorance is bliss!

What is bothersome is that a minority of activists are looking to change tradition, by taking advantage of some people's lack of knowledge and indifference toward Columbus and his legacy of civilization.

Today, this will change because we are going to set Columbus' record straight.

Chapter 1. Hearsay

If you repeat a lie often enough, people will believe it, and sadly, the lies against Columbus, and the anti-Columbus Day movement, are growing, and becoming mainstream:

Snopes says Columbus "didn't discover anything." The New York Times said he was "paranoid, narcissistic," and "ruthless." The Bio Channel says, "he enslaved and mutilated native people." MTV News says, "Columbus was a genocidal rapist." The Huffington Post says, "Columbus supervised the selling of native girls into sexual slavery." The Daily Kos called him a "pirate." [1] Others accused him of being ignorant, racist, a "Nazi" who came here to bring diseases, slavery, and destruction. Just Google search "Christopher Columbus" or "Columbus atro-cities" today, in 2017, and you will see.

I will give the benefit of the doubt that some, or maybe all the companies mentioned above, are just repeating the information they received from "scholars" (or revisionists). My hope is that once the truth of this book is out there, these groups and companies will make retractions or corrections to the Christopher Columbus biography.

Whether in social media, internet memes, blogs, YouTube videos, newspapers, magazines, books or even schools, we are being bombarded with propaganda, and the sad thing is that people are buying it. Like the Bible says, "Faith comes by hearing **and** hearing..." Romans 10:17 (NKJV).

The strategy is clever because, who would promote a holiday for a genocidal rapist? I would be the first person opposing such a thing! Since these accusations come from "scholars" and "historians," and are repeated today by the media, people automatically assume the allegations are true without questioning or taking the time to read the actual primary historical sources.

And the strategy is working; according to The Pew Research Center (2013), "Columbus Day is one of the most inconsistently celebrated U.S. holidays... In recent years, Native American groups and other critics, citing Columbus' own mistreatment of natives and the legacy of European settlement that his voyages initiated –have advocated changing the holiday to something else– perhaps 'Exploration Day.' Minneapolis and Seattle, among other localities, celebrate Indigenous People's [sic] Day instead." [2]

In 2016 Smithsonian said: "Many cities in the United States, and even some states, have in recent years moved to change the focus of Columbus Day off its namesake to the Native Americans who were already living and thriving here prior to Columbus. Berkeley, California, started a movement of cities voting to change Columbus Day to instead celebrate Indigenous Peoples [sic] Day in 1992. Many cities have followed, including Minneapolis-Saint Paul, Minnesota; Seattle, Washington; and Cambridge, Massachusetts. Multiple states also refuse to celebrate Columbus Day, including South Dakota, Hawaii, Alaska and Oregon." [3]

Now, Hawaii is understandable, since Columbus didn't discover it. But the protest didn't stop there; some of these activists are against Thanksgiving Day too. They have their own alternate celebrations like "Unthanksgiving Day" and/or "The National Day of Mourning." [4] Like Columbus, they claim the Pilgrims came to America to bring diseases, slavery, and genocide. And no, I'm not making this up. So, what's next? A protest against the Fourth of July? Should we eliminate Presi-dent's Day too? After all, some of them used to own slaves and killed Indians in war! What about Martin Luther King Jr Day? He committed adultery many times. Should we have an alternate Holiday too? Where should we stop?

The problem with the activists is that their claims are irrational, emotional, and historically inaccurate. These activists are revisionists, and it is a shame that mainstream scholars are not addressing the problem. Some of them ARE the problem. Some of them are the ones spreading the lies.

When it comes to Columbus, we have two camps: One that knows little or nothing about Columbus, which is why so many people are indifferent toward him and what he represents, and the second camp, that think they know something about Columbus (the revisionist version), and now they want to make sure we spell the word **Discover** with quotation marks.

Don't misunderstand me, I don't mind people celebrating Indigenous Peoples' Day as long as it is not the same day or a replacement for Columbus Day, or as long as they don't revise history for anti-American political propaganda gain. If we should not celebrate Columbus, or Columbus Day, because he was involved in war, conquest, and slavery, then by the same token, we should not celebrate Indigenous Peoples' Day, because the natives did the same, and sometimes worse.

They want to shame us for crimes we had nothing to do with; for sins that we don't even practice today! We don't practice slavery, genocide, conquest, or raids. So, why are they so mad again? They foolishly want to give us the impression that we are still living that way today, and we are not. But as I said before, their arguments are irrational.

One thing to notice is that the anti-Columbus supporters make claims without providing any sources, and if they do, they are usually the quotes and opinions from revisionists. If they quote from a historical source, they usually don't give you the chapter or page number, and if they do, the quote is totally out of context. It doesn't take a scholar to find out the truth. All that it takes is curiosity and honesty. If anyone takes the time to read the primary historical sources and compare notes with the claims, it will be obvious the revisionist claims are false and wrong.

In this work, I will provide chapters and page numbers (IN CONTEXT) from the actual primary historical sources, disproving every revision, in the order of Columbus' life and events as they happened. That is, from the time that he was a young man, until the time of his death and beyond.

PS: All **bold letters** and emphasis from quotes are mine, and not from the person who made the statement. Archaic Spanish translations into English are mine too.

Chapter 2. The Historical Sources vs. The Revisionists

Who are the sources, and who are the revisionists? The primary historical sources for Christopher Columbus are:

1. Christopher Columbus- He wrote a few journals, several letters, "The Book of Prophecies," etc.

2. Ferdinand Columbus- He was Columbus' son and accompanied him on his fourth voyage. He wrote his father's biography titled, "The Life of the Admiral Christopher Columbus by his son Ferdinand" also known as the *Historie.*

3. Peter Martyr of Angleria- He was a historian and a contemporary of Columbus. His book is called "De Orbe Novo," which is a collection of letters he wrote as the events were happening or close to the timeline it happened.

4. Bartolomé de las Casas- He was a historian, Dominican Friar, and a contemporary of Columbus. He wrote "Historia de las Indias" Volume 1, 2, and 3 (or more, depending on the publishing house). The English version, "History of the Indies," translated and edited by Andrée M. Collard, is a summary of the original set of volumes. He used Colum-

bus, Ferdinand Columbus, and Peter Martyr as sources for his *Historia*, with the addition of many other documents and his own personal experience and input.

5. Andrés Bernáldez- He was a historian and a contemporary of Columbus. He wrote "Historia de los Reyes Católicos don Fernando y doña Isabel."

6. Antonio de Herrera y Tordesillas- He was a 16th-century chronicler and historian who wrote "Historia general de los hechos de los castellanos en las Islas y Tierra Firme del mar Océano que llaman Indias Occidentales" ("General History of the Deeds of the Castilians on the Islands and Mainland of the Ocean Sea Known as the West Indies"). Though his work was written and published (more or less) a 100 years after the discovery, it is considered to be one of the most complete and best works of its kind.

7. There are also legal papers, official documents, Columbus' testament will, letters from a few other contemporaries, etc.

You can find the works of most of these primary historical sources for free, under public domain, either at your local public library or on the web, in places like Google Books, Internet Archive, Project Gutenberg, etc.

Each of these primary historical sources had a point of view or perspective about the historical events. For example, Columbus told us what he did; Ferdinand Columbus, his son, told us why he did it; Peter Martyr, Andrés Bernáldez, and Herrera told us how Spain saw it, and Bartolomé de las Casas told us how he saw it.

The Modern Historical Revisionists are:

1. Howard Zinn- He was "something of an anarchist." He participated in the activities of various communist organizations. He wrote "A People's History of The United States." He was not a Columbus contemporary, nor a pri-mary source.

2. James W. Loewen- He wrote "Lies My Teacher Told Me," a book that should be renamed as, "Lies Revisionists Told Me." He is not a Columbus contemporary, nor a primary source.

3. Ward Churchill- He is a political activist and co-director of the Denver-based American Indian Movement of Colorado, even though he is not American Indian. Churchill has been a leader of Colorado annual protests against the Columbus Day holiday. [1] He compares Columbus to Heinrich Himmler, a Nazi, even though Columbus didn't commit genocide. [2] Churchill is not a Columbus contemporary, nor a primary source.

4. There are others, but they all repeat the same script. They all share the same or similar profile: that is, they are not the primary historical sources; they are not contemporaries of Columbus; they oppose traditional Judeo-Christian or Western values, and usually they are involved with radical anti-American political groups.

Chapter 3. Discover, not "Discover"

The traditional story of Christopher Columbus tells us that he discovered America. However, revisionists want to discredit Columbus, not only with lies and innuendo but even with semantics! They want us to spell the word **discover** with quotation marks.

When speaking about Columbus (in 2017), The Encyclopedia Britannica website spelled the words **discoverer** and **discovery** with quotation marks.

Columbus "has long been called the '**discoverer**' of the New World, although Vikings such as Leif Eriksson had visited North America five centuries earlier... According to the older understanding, the '**discovery**' of the Americas was a great triumph, one in which Columbus played the part of hero in accomplishing the four voyages." [1]

But when talking about Amerigo Vespucci, the same Encyclopedia Britannica web site spelled the words **discovered, discovery**, and **discoverer** without quotation marks:

Amerigo Vespucci "is believed to have **discovered** the mouth of the Amazon River... The voyage of 1501–02 is of fundamental importance in the history of geographic **discovery** in that Vespucci himself, and scholars as well became convinced that the newly **discovered** lands were not part of Asia but a 'New World' ... the newly **discovered** world be named *'ab Americo Inventore... quasi Americi terram sive Americam'* ('from Amerigo the **discoverer**... as if it were the land of Americus or America')." [2]

Bias? I think so.

In 2016, MTV News said that Christopher Columbus "didn't discover America," that "he landed in the Caribbean and never actually set foot in what is now American soil," and that "the Vikings landed in America almost 500 years before Columbus." [3] But in the next sentence the host blamed Columbus for mistreating native **Americans**. Question: How could Columbus mistreat native AMERICANS, when, according to MTV News, he never discovered the continent or "set foot in what is now American soil"? Contradiction? I think so. And if natives lived on the continent before the Vikings, then by the same faulty logic they didn't discover America either! In addition, Columbus indeed discovered the Central and South American part of the continent, even though he never reached North America.

The question is, how can Columbus be responsible for any conflicts in places he never reached, or places he never discovered or settled? The problem is that there is a big misunderstanding with the word **Discover**. The word **Discover** never meant "the first person to find desolate land" in Columbus' historical context. If Columbus was looking for a straight route to the Asian continent (for trade and to send missionaries to the "Great Khan") then that means he was looking for inhabited land.

From Columbus' own journal:

In that same month, on the information which I had given Your Majesties about the lands of India and a **ruler** known as the Great Khan (which means in Spanish 'King of Kings').

Note: A ruler rules over **people**! Columbus continued:

... Your Majesties... send me, Christopher Columbus, to those lands of India to meet **their rulers**
and to see the **towns** and lands and their
distribution, and all other things, and to find out in
what manner they might be converted to our Holy
Faith; and you ordered me not to go eastward by
land, as is customary, but to take my course westward, **where, so far as we know, no man has
travelled before today** (*The Voyage of Christopher Columbus,* translated by John Cummins, Pro-
logue, p. 81).

Columbus was looking for land already populated. This is
what primary historical source, Bartolomé de las Casas, wrote:

... I understand that when he tried to find a Christian Prince to sponsor him, he was already sure that
he would **discover** [new] lands and **peoples** in it...
**Columbus did not name it the Indies beca-
use it had already been seen or discovered
by others**, but because it was the eastern part of
India ultra Gangem which, going East, was to the
west of us since the world is round. No cosmographer had ever marked out the boundaries of
India except those of the ocean (*Historia de las Indias* by Las Casas, Cap. V. Translation into English
is mine. See *History of the Indies* by Las Casas,
Book One, Ch. 5, pp. 20-21).

"India" was another word for Asia in Columbus' time.
Some people might be offended that Columbus called the natives,
"Indians," when they were not in "India," or Asia. But Columbus
might not be as wrong, as some may think, because those who

were living in America before Columbus, somehow came here from "India," or the Asian continent. I wonder why some people might be offended with Columbus calling the natives, "Indians," but they are okay with the name, "Americans," when that was not the name of the continent either! The name "America" came as a consequence of Columbus' discoveries, and Amerigo Vespucci (where the name "America" comes from) was a contemporary of Columbus as well.

All that Columbus wanted was to go straight from Spain to Asia, instead of sailing around Africa, like the Europeans were doing. That's basic children's school history. I can't believe some people forgot that! Columbus knew Asian land was already discovered by Asians, and he knew Europeans had traded there, which also means he was not looking to be the first European to reach India or Asia because again, he already knew Europeans had reached it. He was inspired by the travels of Marco Polo, so he knew a European already had reached China, in Asia. [4] Therefore, those who bring Vikings to the conversation, don't know or understand what the word **Discover**, or its historical context, means.

That's why it doesn't matter if Columbus knew about the Vikings reaching North America or not, because Columbus was aiming South, toward India, but also with the purpose of exploring the South Asian lands and islands Europeans had not reached yet, where, like Las Casas said, "no cosmographer had ever marked out the boundaries." But of course, Columbus was not in South Asia, but in the Caribbean, and later in Central and South America. This makes him the first European to reach those places at such a time.

What did Columbus discover?

1. Columbus discovered and proved that one can sail safely and straight from Spain (or Europe) to the other side.

2. Because of him, and him alone, it was later discovered that they were on another continent, and not in Asia.

3. Columbus is the one who brought two different worlds back together, after hundreds of years of lost communication.

4. He, and those who followed after him, discovered people and lands the Old Word did not know existed.

5. Columbus was the first European to explore the Caribbean, and probably the first European to reach Central America, including Honduras, Nicaragua, Costa Rica, Panamá and Venezuela in South America.

To those who still insist Columbus didn't discover anything, who want to discredit Columbus' accomplishments by playing semantic games blended with ignorance; to those of you who say, the "Native Americans" were the ones who discovered America because they were here first, I want to ask you the following questions:

1. What was the name of the native person who reached American land first?
2. What native tribe discovered America?
3. What year?
4. When?
5. How did they get there?
6. What country did they come from?
7. Where did they settle first? North, South or Central America?

The fact is we don't know the answers to those questions, but we know the answers to the same questions when we are talking about Christopher Columbus.

As for the Vikings, they sailed from Iceland and Greenland, which are very close to North America, while Columbus sailed straight west from Spain (and the Canary Islands) to America, which was farther and something people would not have dared to do back in those days. In fact, Columbus' sailors were in tears, scared to death, as they left the Old World into the unknown. There were times they thought they were going to die. See *The Life of the Admiral Christopher Columbus* by his son Ferdinand, Ch. 18, p. 48.

The Vikings quickly left America, not knowing they were on another continent. But if the Vikings would have stayed there, impacting history as Columbus did, we would still be hearing the same complaints anyway. Remember, the Vikings were white, which is a crime to some revisionists; they also practiced conquest, war, raids, slavery, and rape. But the worst "crime" of all, was that the Viking who presumably reached America, Leif Erikson, was a Christian! [5] Can you imagine the reaction revisionists might have once they find out this! They might stop bragging that the Vikings were the first doing anything! They might have a heart attack! They hate that "crime" more than any other. Like I said before, we would be still hearing the same objections today! On the other hand, I don't know why some people want to magnify the Vikings' discoveries, which had no impact historically, and diminish Columbus' discoveries, which have an actual historical impact.

In the words of Thomas A. Bowden, "Columbus did discover America--- for Europe. Prior to 1492, Europeans lived in total ignorance of the Western hemisphere and the people who inhabited it. Columbus and those who follow him lift that cover of ignorance--- they *'dis-covered'* America. Once this knowledge had kindled Europe's interest in the New World, European colonists came in growing numbers, bringing with them the wisdom of Western civilization in a vast westward movement, laying the groundwork for mankind's greatest political and economic achievement, the United States of America. Seen in this light, Columbus's voyage is the one that truly made a difference historically." [6]

And "it is significant that one never hears condemnation of the Vikings, or the Chinese, Japanese, Irish, or Welsh, or any other purported pre-Columbian voyagers, for having inaugurated centuries of 'ecocide' and genocide. By focusing all their attention on Columbus, his enemies confess their agreement that his voyage was the only one that mattered." [7]

I would add that we are here in the New World today BECAUSE of Columbus and Columbus alone. Not because of natives, Vikings or anyone else, but because of Christopher Columbus.

Chapter 4. The Christ Bearer

Columbus was a Genoese, which all primary historical sources and contemporaries confirmed. Even this is an argument to some revisionists. Those who won't accept this fact are not real historians, but conspiracy theorists. Columbus himself said so in a letter. He wrote, "Genoa... from there I came and from there I was born (*Relaciones y Cartas de Cristóbal Colón*, p. 254). See also *History of the* Indies by Las Casas, p. 15; *De Orbe Novo* by Peter Martyr, The First Decade, Book I, p. 57; *Historia de los Reyes Católicos* by Andrés Bernáldez, Tomo I, Cap. CXVIII, p. 269; *Historia General* by Herrera, Década I, Lib. I, Cap. VII, p. 11; *Historia General y Natural* by Oviedo, Cap. II, p. 12, and *Christoper Columbus The Grand Design* by Taviani, Chapters II and III.

Columbus was also a man of faith. Spreading the Gospel was one of his main purposes for his voyages. That explains why the New World today is mostly Catholic or Protestant and not Islamic, Buddhist, or Hindu. That also explains why some places Columbus discovered have religious names like San Salvador, which means "Holy Savior;" Trinidad which accordingly means "Trinity," as the Holy Trinity. San Juan, today known as Puerto Rico, means "Saint John," in honor of John the Baptist; Santo Domingo (the capital of the Dominican Republic), meaning "Holy Sunday," and so on.

Primary historical source, Peter Martyr wrote:

A certain Christopher Columbus, a Genoese, proposed to the Catholic King and Queen, Ferdinand and

Isabella, **to discover the islands which touch the Indies,** by sailing from the western extremity of this country. He asked for ships and whatever was necessary to navigation, promising not only **to propagate the Christian religion,** but also certainly to bring back pearls, spices and gold beyond anything ever imagined (*De Orbe Novo* by Peter Martyr, The First Decade, Book I, p. 57).

Columbus believed he was chosen by Providence to fulfill prophetic Scriptures. He said:

God Our Lord with a palpable hand opened my understanding that it was feasible to sail from here to the Indies and placed in me a great desire to execute it. Filled with this burning desire, I came to your highnesses... (*Historia del Almirante,* Cap. IV. Translation into English is mine. See also *The Life of the Admiral Christopher Columbus* by his son Ferdinand, Ch. 4, p. 10).

I have already said that for the execution of the enterprise of the Indies neither intelligence nor mathematics nor world maps were of any use to me; it was the fulfillment of Isaiah's prophecy (*Colección de los Viajes* by Navarrete, Tomo II, p. 295. Translation into English is mine).

Columbus believed he fulfilled Bible prophecies like: But I know their works, and their thoughts: I come that I may gather them together with all nations and tongues: and they shall come and shall see my glory. And I will set a sign among them, and I will send of them that shall be saved, to the Gentiles into the sea, into Africa, and Lydia them that draw the bow: into Italy, and Greece, to the islands afar off, **to them that have not heard of me, and have not seen my glory**... (Isaiah 66:18-19. Latin Vulgate).

Cynics had said Columbus was a self-proclaimed messiah, [1] or that he was trying to appeal to the Queen of Spain, who was deeply religious as well. That could not be further from the truth. Columbus never claimed to be a messiah, and his life was consistently spiritual, even to the day he died. His last words were the last words of Jesus on the cross, "Lord, into your hands I commit my spirit." Columbus died on the Day of the Ascension.

Columbus' son, Ferdinand, described him as "so observant of the matters of religion that in fasting and in praying the Divine Office, he might be taken for a member of a religious order, and so much an enemy of swearing and blasphemy he was, that I swear that I never heard him utter an oath other than 'by St. Fernando!' " *Historia del Almirante,* Cap. III, pp. 14-15. Translation into English is mine. See *The Life of the Admiral Christopher Columbus* by his son Ferdinand, Ch. 3, p. 9.

... he confessed and received communion frequently; he recited the canonical hours like an ecclesiastic or a monk; most inimical to blasphemies and oaths, he was most devoted to Our Lady and to the seraphic Father, St. Francis... most jealous of the Divine honor, eager and desirous for the conversion of these peoples, and that the faith of Jesus Christ should be everywhere spread, and singularly given and devoted to God that he might be made worthy to help in some way to win the Holy

Sepulcher. Patient, long-suffering, prone to forgive injuries, Columbus was a man of courageous soul and high aspirations, always pervaded with infinite confidence in Divine Providence and never failing in loyalty to the sovereigns whom he served. [2]

He met his wife in a church in Portugal, and years later he left his son under the care of church clerics, after his wife died, while he pursued his enterprise with the Spanish Sovereigns. See *The Life of the Admiral Christopher Columbus* by his son Ferdinand, Ch. 5, p. 14 and Ch. 12, p. 37.

After one of his voyages "Columbus went ashore at Cadiz" where "he adopted the coarse brown habit of a Minorite friar, which remained his usual costume when in Spain. Apparently he believed that his misfortunes were chastisements of divine providence for his pride, and so laid off the costly apparel proper to an Admiral of the Ocean Sea, and assumed the humble garb of his Franciscan friends as evidence of repentance and humility. Columbus found his most loyal friends ashore among ecclesiastics, especially those in monastic orders. He liked their piety, their conversation, and their simple way of living; and in his travels about Spain he preferred the hospitality of a monastery to that of caballero or grandee." [3]

Columbus was Catholic. There was no Protestant Church back then. However, Martin Luther was a contemporary of his, and the Protestant Reformation came 11 years after Columbus' death, spreading the gospel to both the Old and the New World.

When it comes to education, Columbus wasn't illiterate either:

As a child, his parents made him learn to read and write, and he learned such calligraphy... that he could have made a living by it. He also studied arithmetic and drawing with the same skill and degree of excellence. He studied Latin... the *Historia portuguesa* praises him as a good Latinist-which must have given him an unusual insight into human and divine affairs. Since God endowed him with good judgment, a sound memory and eagerness to learn, he sought the company of learned men and applied himself to his studies with great intensity, acquiring proficiency in geometry, geography, cosmography, astrology or astronomy, and seamanship (*History of the Indies* by Las Casas, Book One, Ch. 3, p. 15).

It cannot be a coincidence that his name, Christopher, means in Greek, the "Christ-bearer;" while his last name, Columbus, means "Dove." Ferdinand Columbus wrote:

... we will have to say that he was truly Colombo, or 'Paloma' [Dove] since he brought the grace of the Holy Spirit to the New World ... and consequently, his surname 'Colón' [Columbus] which he revived, was a fitting one since in the Greek it means 'member,' being his own name 'Cristobal' [Christopher], people may know who he was a member of; that is, of Christ, of whom he was to be sent for the salvation of those people... (*Historia del Almirante*, Cap. I, pp. 5-6. Translation into English is mine. See *The Life of the Admiral Christopher Columbus* by his son Ferdinand, Ch. 1, p. 4).

I'm convinced this is one of the main reasons why revisionists hate Columbus so much. They hate him because of the

Judeo-Christian values he brought. Remember, many of these anti-Columbus propagandists are secularists who don't like religion or the traditional values of our culture. In fact, I remember reading a comment by a young person in social media, who said that now that he knows "the real story of Columbus" (i.e. the revisionist version), he doesn't want to celebrate Columbus Day, nor any other American holiday, because "America's moral founding and the Christian religion are flawed and evil." That's exactly what revisionists want us to think! They want us to associate Columbus, Christianity, and Western civilization, with everything that went wrong during Columbus' time, or everything that is wrong, today, in our society. Either way, they are wrong.

Chapter 5. Pirate of the Caribbean

"Columbus was a pirate" [1] is the least popular accusation out there but is still worth it to mention and discredit. This "pirate" episode supposedly took place when he was a young man, long before his discoveries.

"History of the Indies" by Bartolomé de las Casas, translated by Andrée M. Collard, Book One, Chapter 4, p. 18, says that Columbus accompanied a relative of his, named Colombo Junior, or The Younger, who was a "pirate." The problem is that the original Spanish language says Colombo The Younger was a corsair ("corsario") and not a pirate ("pirata"). Benjamin Keen translated the word correctly in *The Life of the Admiral Christopher Columbus* by his son Ferdinand (Chapter 5), which is where Las Casas took the story from.

The difference between a 15th or 16th-century pirate and a corsair is that a pirate is a criminal who plunders at sea, while a corsair is any individual granted a license by their government to attack ships belonging to an enemy government, usually during a war.

Columbus' son, Ferdinand, claimed his father was with corsair Colombo The Younger, fighting against four Venetian galleys that were returning from Flanders, and during the fight, ships from both sides caught on fire and sunk, but Columbus survived by swimming to the Portuguese shore, wounded. [2]

The problem with that story is that even though it happened, Columbus wasn't there. The event took place in 1485

AFTER Columbus had left Portugal for Spain. [3] In other words, Columbus wasn't accompanying Colombo The Younger at that time. Nevertheless, the combat that wounded Columbus, as he swam to the shores of Portugal, did happen, but rather at an earlier time.

Benjamin Keen says Ferdinand confused the event with another combat that took place in 1476 "between a convoy of five Genoese vessels and a French armada, commanded by the corsair Guillaume de Casenove. Morison, and more recently the Italian scholar Emilio Taviani, believe that Columbus shipped aboard one of the Genoese vessels as a common sailor and accepted the authenticity of the story that he was cast ashore in Portugal, as told by Ferdinand." [4]

The closest thing of Columbus himself acting as a corsair was when he was probably 21 years old, in 1472. According to Columbus, the King of Naples, René of Anjou, sent him to Tunis to capture a galleass named "Fernandina." But it's clear Columbus was not a pirate, and when he fought in 1476 against Casenove, he did as a common sailor in self-defense. See *The Life of the Admiral Christopher* Columbus by his son Ferdinand, Ch. 4, p. 11.

Chapter 6. The Flat Earth

In the past, we were led to believe Columbus was ridiculed for trying to prove the Earth was round, but today we are told that is not true. Now we are told that "most educated Europeans already believed the Earth as round. In fact, it was an idea that had been established by the Ancient Greeks..." [1]

Others will highlight the fact that Columbus was wrong about the size of the Earth, while the "wise men" from Spain were right, believing the Earth was bigger. The purpose of this half-truth and innuendo is to portray Columbus as a fool who didn't know anything, and that he didn't face opposition and mockery, like the traditional story tells us about. The fact is, the Spanish council ridiculed Columbus and they believed in all sorts of myths as well. Ships back then didn't have the technology we have today; sailing long distances meant that they would quickly run out of provisions and people would die. That's why the Spanish council believed Columbus' enterprise wouldn't succeed.

This is what Peter Martyr had to say about the issue:

> ... although the opinion of Columbus seems to be contradictory to the theories of the ancients concerning **the size of the globe** and its circumnavigation, the birds and many other objects brought thence seem to indicate that these islands do belong, be it by proximity or by their products, to

India (*De Orbe Novo* by Peter Martyr, The First Decade, Book I, p. 65).

The council was right that the Earth was bigger and not smaller like Columbus thought. But Columbus was right that he would make it safe to the other side in a short period of time, as he did in 1492. However, neither Columbus, nor the Spanish council, knew that there was a continent between Europe and Asia, which is something that makes Columbus' discovery more remarkable. Revisionist writer, Howard Zinn, said: "For, like other informed people of his time, he knew the world was round and he could sail west in order to get to the Far East." [2] Except that Europeans wouldn't dare to sail west, due to the afore-mentioned reasons.

Now let's read primary historical source Bartolomé de las Casas, and see what the "informed people of his time" believed, and how they ridiculed Columbus:

> He arrived on January 20, 1485, and began his own terrible, continuous, painful and tedious battle, perhaps harsher and more horrible than a battle with material weapons. That is, to inform many people who did not understand him, even though they presumed they did. And to answer and tolerate many who shunned him and did not care about him, receiving insults that pained him very much... Columbus would present his proposal, giving reasons and authoritative support to prove it feasible... some would ask how it was possible that after thousands of years no one had heard about those Indies, and if they existed, how was it that the famous Ptolemy and the many other astrologers and wise men, all of whom had written about such

things, wrote nothing about the Indies... others argued in the following manner: that the world was infinite, therefore it would not be possible after many years of sailing to reach the eastern limits, as Columbus proposed, from the west... If it was navigable, it was doubtful that there was land or inhabited land, on the other side. But if they were inhabited, it was unlikely that one could set out to find it... Those who showed to be more knowledgeable on the subject of mathematics, related to astrology and cosmography, said that from this small sphere of water and land, there was just a very small part uncovered, because everything else was covered with water, and therefore it was not possible to navigate, except through the banks or coasts... And they said more: sailing straight West, as Columbus proposed, would mean one could never return, for supposing the world were round, going West was sinking downhill out of the hemisphere described by Ptolemy; it would be necessary to return uphill, which is something ships cannot do... others brought other arguments not worth recording... (*Historia de las Indias* by Las Casas, Cap. XXIX. Translation into English is mine. See *History of the Indies* by Las Casas, Book One, Ch. 29, pp. 26-28).

Consider this: if the shape of the Earth was a settled argument, why then did some of the Spanish council members "argue that the world was infinite"? "Infinite" sounds more like a flat surface than a round shape. Don't you think? I could be wrong, but it's clear the shape of the Earth was not the reason they rejected Columbus' project. However, "most educated Europeans believing the Earth was not flat," also means some educated Europeans, perhaps, believed that it was flat. What does that tell you about the common folk?

If the shape of the Earth was **settled**, and the evidence was **conclusive**, why then did Columbus doubt its shape during his third voyage?

Columbus said:

> I have now seen so much irregularity, that I have come to another conclusion respecting the earth, namely, that it is **not round** as they describe, but of the form of a pear, which is very round except where the stalk grows, at which part it is most prominent; or like a round ball, upon one part of which is a prominence like a woman's nipple, this protrusion being the highest and nearest the sky, situated under the equinoctial line, and at the eastern extremity of this sea,—I call that the eastern extremity, where the land and the islands end (*Select Letters of Christopher Columbus*, p. 134).

If the shape of the Earth was settled, why then did 16th-century priest, Father José de Acosta, argue about the shape of the Earth, in his *Natural & Moral History* book, and he used the "Victoria" Spanish ship that successfully circumnavigated the world with Magellan as evidence of the roundness of the Earth? The following is **an archaic English** translation of what he wrote:

> Who will not confesse but the ship called the Victories (worthie doubtlesse of eternall memorie) hath wonne the honor and praise to have best disco-

vered and compassed the round earth, yea, that great Chaos and infinite Vast which the ancient Philosophers affirmed to bee vnder the Magellan's ship, which is represented on the covers of the volumes earth, having compassed about the worlde and circled the vastnesse of the great Oceans. Who is hee then that will not confesse by this Navigation but the whole earth (although it were bigger then it is described) is subiect to the feet of man, seeing he may measure it? Thus, without doubt, the Heaven is of a round and perfect figure; and the earth likewise imbracing and ioyning with the water makes one globe or round bowle framed of these two elements, having their bounds and limits within their own roundnes and greatnes (*The Natural & Moral History of the Indies* by Jose de Acosta, Ch. 1, pp. 4-5).

Columbus wasn't trying to prove the Earth was round, but he decided to cross the ocean BECAUSE the Earth is round. He "considered that since all the water and land of the world constituted and formed a sphere, it would be possible to go around it from east to west, men walking in it until they could be foot to foot at opposite ends with each other wherever they were placed [on Earth] ..." *Historia del Almirante*, Cap. VI, p. 27. Translation into English is mine. See *The Life of the Admiral Christopher Columbus* by his son Ferdinand, Ch. 6, p. 15.

Again, I'm not saying the council refused Columbus' proposal because of the shape of the Earth. What I'm saying is that the Earth's shape issue was not settled yet.

Now, let's see how arrogant "the professionals" were with Columbus. They told him that "those lands had remained unknown to innumerable **learned men and experts** in navigation; and it was most unlikely that the Admiral should know more than all other men."

How condescending! Some "doubted that it could be navigated... they questioned whether habitable lands existed at the other end... In the end, then, they condemned the enterprise as **vain and impossible**..." *The Life of the Admiral Christopher Columbus* by his son Ferdinand, Ch. 12, p. 39.

Columbus wrote, "all those who learned of my enterprise rejected it, mocking and laughing at it." *Historia del Almirante,* Cap. IV, p. 17. Translation into English is mine. See *The Life of the Admiral Christopher Columbus* by his son Ferdinand, Ch. 4, p. 10.

Some in the present have accused Columbus of "incomplete and faulty grasp of classical learning." [3] But the man who "knew less" than the "learned men and experts," was the one who proved everyone wrong. While the "professionals" were comfortable in Spain mocking Columbus, it was he who risked his life and succeeded when he was told, "you can't do it."

The Bible says, "But God chose the foolish things of the world to shame the wise; God chose the weak things of the world to shame the strong." 1 Corinthians 1: 27 (NIV).

Years later, Columbus responded to his critics in a similar manner, by saying:

> Perhaps Your Highnesses and all the others who know me and to whom this letter may be shown will criticize me in various ways, publicly or privately, as an uneducated man, an uninformed sailor, an ordinary person, etc. I respond with the words of Saint Matthew: 'Oh, Lord, how many things you have kept secret from the wise and have made known to the innocent!' And again from Saint Matthew, as our Lord entered Jerusalem, the chil-

dren sang, 'Hosanna, son of David!' In order to test him, the scribes asked him if he had heard what they were saying; and he answered that he had, saying, 'Don't you know that truth comes from the mouths of innocent children.' Or consider the apostles, who wrote such profound things, in particular St. John, 'In the beginning was the Word, and the Word was God,' etc.; such great words from uneducated men (*Colección de los Viajes* by Navarrete, Tomo II, p. 293. Translation into English is mine).

In conclusion, though Columbus wasn't trying to prove the roundness of the Earth, the traditional story of Columbus still stands: The Spanish council ridiculed him, but in the end, Columbus proved all their myths wrong.

Chapter 7. Mutiny

The traditional story of Columbus tells us that the sailors murmured against him in almost a mutinous way, as they were on their way to discover the New World, during his first voyage. However, revisionist author James Loewen wrote that "to make a better myth, six of twelve [school] textbooks exaggerate the crew's complaints into a near-mutiny. The primary sources differ. Some claim the sailors threatened to go back home if they didn't reach land soon. Other sources claim that Columbus lost heart and that the captains of the other two ships persuaded him to keep on. Still, other sources suggest that the three leaders met and agreed to continue on for a few more days and then reassess the situation." [1]

Notice, he didn't provide the name of the alleged sources. Let's read what the actual historical sources have to say starting with Columbus:

> They could contain themselves no longer, and be-gan to complain of the length of the voyage. I encouraged them as best I could, trying to raise their hopes of the benefits they might gain from it. I also told them that it was useless to complain; having set out for the Indies I shall continue this voyage until, with God's grace, I reach them (*Columbus' Journal*, translated by John Cummins, Wednesday, October 10, 1492).

That doesn't sound like someone who "lost heart" and wanted to return back to Spain!

> ... and being the Admiral a foreigner and without favor [at the Spanish Court], and his opinion condemned and despised by so many learned and wise men, he would have no one to defend him and and all would believe what they [the Court] said, blaming him of ineptitude and ignorance to whatever he might say to justify himself. And there were some who said that in order to solve the problem **they should throw him into the sea if he would not turn back, reporting that he fell while looking at the stars and sky**, and none would question their story. That was the best means of assuring their safe return. In this way they continued the journey, murmuring, grumbling and plotting every day. The Admiral became aware of their faithlessness and the wicked intentions they had against him. Therefore, he sometimes addressed them with fair words and at other times very passionately, **as if fearless of death**, threatened them with what kind of punishment he would use if they hindered the voyage. This way he somewhat calmed their fears and machinations. To bolster their hopes, he reminded them of the signs [of land] they had seen, promising them that they would find some land in a short period of time (*Historia del Almirante*, Cap. XIX, p. 90. Translation into English is mine. See The Life *of the Admiral Christopher Columbus* by his son Ferdinand, Ch. 20, pp. 52-53).

His companions began to murmur in secret, for at first they concealed their discontent, but soon, openly, desiring to get rid of their leader, whom **they even planned to throw into the sea.** They considered that they had been deceived by this Genoese, who was leading them to some place from whence they could never return. After the thirtieth day they angrily demanded that he should turn back and go no farther; Columbus, by using gentle words, holding out promises and flattering their hopes, sought to gain time, and he succeeded in calming their fears; finally also reminding them that if they refused him their obedience or attempted violence against him, they would be accused of treason by their sovereigns (*De Orbe Novo* by Peter Martyr, The First Decade, Book I, pp. 59-60).

Las Casas, in its Spanish version said:

... y comenzaron a murmurar sobre el viaje, y de quien en él los había puesto... empezaron a manifestar, y a desvergonzadamente decirle en la cara que los había engañado y los llevaba perdidos para matarlos, y juraban a tal o cual cosa, que si no regresaba, lo primero que harían era arrojarlo al mar... con palabras muy dulces y amorosas... los esforzaba, animaba, y rogaba... Con estas y otras palabras él hizo lo que pudo hacer de su parte ... [2]

Translation:

... and they began to murmur about the journey, and about the one who had put them in it... they shamelessly told him, in his face, that he had deceived them and had led them to their death; **they swore that they would throw him into the sea if he would not turn back**... With very sweet and loving words... he encouraged them, motivated them, and pleaded with them... with these and other words he tried to do what he could...

Las Casas also said that the stories of Columbus fainting and losing heart, were false. See *Historia de las Indias* by Las Casas, Tomo I, Lib. I, Cap. XXXIX, p. 290.

From Herrera's archaic Spanish version:

... tanto más se acrecentaba el miedo de la gente, y tomaban ocasión de murmurar... que para quitar contiendas, era mejor echarlo a la mar con disimulación, y decir que desgraciadamente se había caído mientras estaba embebido en considerar las estrellas... Cristóbal... a veces con buenas palabras, y otras advirtiendo del castigo que se les daría si le impidiesen el viaje... [3]

Translation:

... all the more, people's fear increased and they took the opportunity to murmur... that, **in order to solve the problem, it was better to throw him into the sea**, and say that he, unfortunately, fell while he was distracted looking at the stars... Columbus... sometimes spoke to them with kind words, and at others, he warned them of the punishment they would receive if they prevented the voyage...

I don't know what Mr. Loewen is talking about! All these sources say the same thing. That is, that they murmured, they complained in his face, they threatened to throw him overboard if he wouldn't return, and that Columbus replied to them with kind words and with words of warning of coming punishments if they were to harm him. How can a death threat be an EXAGGERATION of "near mutiny"?

This is also one of the reasons why Columbus kept false entries in his log; in order that his superstitious mutinous crew would not panic about how far they were from home. See *The Life of the Admiral Christopher Columbus* by his son Ferdinand, Ch. 18, p. 48.

However, Mr. Loewen claims in his book that during "the return voyage, Columbus confided in his journal the real reason for the false entries: he wanted to keep the route to the Indies secret. As paraphrased by Las Casas, 'He says that he pretended to have gone a greater distance in order to confound the pilots and sailors who did the charts, that he remain master of the route to the Indies.' " [4]

SO? The King of Portugal tried to steal his route at one point. [5] What was wrong with Columbus protecting his project? After all, he was accountable to the King and Queen of Spain alone. He was not accountable to sailors, pilots or other countries.

Chapter 8. First to See Land

Revisionists give grief against Columbus, even in minor points. There was a reward to the first person to sight land, and even though Columbus didn't cry, "land, land!" he ended up winning it, during his first voyage. Revisionists assert that this was greed. What revisionists won't tell you is that some of the crew had cried "land! land!" before a new land was ever found. I wonder why revisionists won't charge these people with greed too!

Columbus' son explains:

> The Sunday after, on October 7, at sunrise, a sign of land was seen towards the west: but because it was dark, no one dared to become the author of such novelty, not because of the shame of being wrong, but for the fear of losing the reward of 30 escudos [or 10,000 maravedis] income granted by the Catholic Kings to those who first would see land. Because as stated before, in order to prevent unjustified feelings of joy, it was forbidden, with the penalty to lose it [the reward] if they cried 'land' without evidence of it in the term of three days, even if they later see it, it would still be considered false news. For this reason, those of the Admiral's ship were afraid, not wanting to risk saying 'land, land' (*Historia del Almirante*, Cap. XX, p. 96. Trans-

lation into English is mine. See *The Life of the Admiral Christopher Columbus* by his son Ferdinand, Ch. 21, p. 56).

Ferdinand Columbus continues:

[The land] was first sight by Rodrigo de Triana, a sailor, and it was two leagues of distance away; but the reward of the 30 escudos was not granted to him, but to the Admiral, who first saw the light in the darkness of the night, signifying the spiritual light which he was to introduce in that darkness (*Historia del Almirante*, Cap. XXI, 101. Translation into English is mine. See *The Life of the Admiral Christopher Columbus* by his son Ferdinand, Ch. 22, pp. 58-59).

What "light" was Ferdinand talking about? Here is Columbus' own testimony:

I was on the poop deck at ten o'clock in the evening when I saw a light. It was so indistinct that I could not be sure it was land, but I called Pedro Gutierrez, the Butler of the King's Table, and told him to look at what I thought was a light. He looked, and saw it. I also told Rodrigo Sanchez de Segovia, Your Majesties' observer on board, but he saw nothing because he was standing in the wrong place. After I had told them, the light appeared once or twice more, like a wax candle rising and falling. Only a few people thought it was a sign of land, but I was sure we were close to a landfall. Then the Pinta, being faster and in the lead, sighted land and made the signal as I had ordered. The first man to sight land was called Rodrigo de Triana (*Columbus' Journal, translated* by John Cummins, Thursday, October 11, 1492).

Columbus had witnesses that saw the light of the land with him, but it was the Spanish king and queen who wanted to award Columbus instead.

The Sovereigns awarded it to the Admiral, because the light seen first by him was believed to have been on land (*The Journal of Christopher Columbus,* translated by Clements R. Markham, p. 36, Footnote 1).

The quote above is from a footnote on Antonio de Herrera's *Historia.* (*Historia General,* Década I, Lib. I, Cap. XII, p. 20).

More interesting is that Bartolomé de las Casas, who was Columbus' contemporary, and sometimes his harshest critic, believed it was fair for the king and queen to award Columbus, and not Rodrigo de Triana. In his archaic Spanish, he wrote:

La tierra fue vista primero por un marinero llamado Rodrigo de Triana, pero los 10,000 maravedís prometidos, los recibió Cristóbal Colón por sentencia de los reyes, juzgando que como él había visto primero la lumbre, él también había visto primero la tierra.

Translation:

A sailor named Rodrigo de Triana saw the land first, but the kings granted the promised 10,000 maravedis to Christopher Columbus, judging that he saw the light of the land first.

He continues:

Donde podemos ver que esto no es poca cosa, la bondad y la justicia de Dios, que en este mundo Él recompensa y también castiga, en acuerdo a las obras y virtudes solicitadas en cada uno de nosotros, responden a la confianza de su providencia; Él ordenó, que como Cristóbal Colón llevó la parte más laboriosa y angustiosa de todo el viaje; como él personalmente sufrió la carga de todas las personas, el desprecio, los problemas y aflicciones que muchas veces le causaron; dado que solo él tuvo fe perseverante en la providencia divina, confiando que al final él no iba a ser defraudado, él obtuvo este favor, y se le atribuyó haber visto la tierra por primera vez, al ver la luz, que era un símbolo espiritual, de alguien que con su sudor y trabajo infundió a Cristo en aquellas personas que vivían en una oscuridad tan profunda, y así gozase de la merced de los 10,000 maravedís; que es de estimar, no tanto por el valor de ellos, como algo tan poco, sino por la alegría y el consuelo que en esta vida, aunque temporal, le favoreció y le otorgó. [1]

Translation:

Where we can see this is no small matter, the goodness and justice of God, who in this world He rewards and also punishes, as the works and virtues requested on each one of us, respond to the confidence toward His providence. He ordained that since Christopher Columbus carried the most laborious and anguished part of the whole voyage; since he personally suffered the burden of all the people, their contempt, trouble and afflictions that many times they caused him; since he alone had persevering faith in divine providence, he was not going to be defrauded in the end; he gained this favor, and was credited with having first seen the land by first seeing the light, which was a spiritual symbol, of one who by his sweat and labors, infused Christ into those people who lived in such deep darkness, and so enjoyed the mercy of the 10,000 maravedis; which is to esteem, not so much for the value of them, as something so little, but for the joy and consolation which in this life, even though temporal, favored and granted him.

Remember, this was the same mutinous crew who gave Columbus a hard time; from the sailors who threatened his life, to the captain who later deserted him out of greed; to those who disobeyed him and shipwrecked the Santa María caravel during this first voyage, as we are going to see later in Chapter 14.

I don't know why revisionists would give grief over minor things like this, especially since the decision came from the King and Queen of Spain, and not from somebody else. The king and queen had the last word.

Chapter 9. Thanking God First

When Columbus discovered America on October 12th, 1492, the first thing he did was to give thanks to God. However, James Loewen protested saying: "Most of them [school textbooks] tell us that Columbus's first act after going ashore was 'thanking God for leading them safely across the sea'- even though the surviving summary of Columbus's own journal states only that 'before them all, he took possession of the island, as in fact he did, for the King and Queen, his Sovereigns.' " [1]

Yet, when talking about Bartolomé de las Casas, Mr. Loewen says: "Las Casas, the first <u>great</u> historian of the Americas, **who relied on primary materials** and helped preserve them." [2]

So, let's see what, in Loewen's own words, "the first great historian" (who also wrote a copy of Columbus' own journal) had to say about this particular episode. From Las Casas' archaic Spanish version account:

> El Almirante tomó la bandera real, y los dos capitanes tomaron las banderas con la cruz verde, que el Almirante mantuvo en todos los barcos como símbolo e insignia, con una F, que representa al rey Fernando, y una I por la reina doña Isabel, y por encima de cada letra, su corona respectiva ... Saltando a tierra, el Almirante y todos los demás se arrodillaron, muchos de ellos derramando lágri-

mas, dando muchas gracias al Señor Dios Todopoderoso por traerlos a todos a salvo ... luego el
Almirante ... tomó posesión de la isla mencionada
... [3]

Translation:

The Admiral took the royal flag, and the two
Captains took the flags with the green cross, which
the Admiral kept on all ships as symbol and motto
with an F, which stands for King Ferdinand, and the
I for Queen Isabel, and on top of each letter, a
respective crown... Jumping ashore, the Admiral
and everyone else kneeled down, many of them
shedding tears, giving many thanks to the Lord God
almighty for bringing them all safe... **then** the
Admiral... took possession of the said island...

Let's read Herrera's archaic Spanish version account too:

... el Almirante, con la barca armada, y el estandarte
Real tendido, salió a tierra, y lo mismo hicieron los
capitanes Martín Alonso Pinzón, y Vicente Yañez
Pinzón, con las banderas de la empresa, que era una
cruz verde, con ciertas coronas, y los nombres de los
reyes católicos. Habiendo todos besado la tierra, y
arrodillados, dado gracias a Dios, con lágrimas, por
la gracia que les había hecho, el Almirante se
levantó, y llamó San Salvador a aquella Isla... y con
la solemnidad, y palabras necesarias, tomó la
posesión en nombre de los reyes católicos... [4]

Translation:

The Admiral came ashore with an armed boat, and the royal standard; Captains Martín Alonso Pinzón and Vicente Yáñez Pinzón did the same with the banners of the expedition, which had a green cross, certain crowns, and the names of the Catholic Kings. Having all of them kissed the land, they knelt, giving thanks to God with tears, for the grace granted to them. The Admiral stood up, and called the island San Salvador [Holy Savior] ... and with solemnity and ceremony, he took possession of it in the name of the Catholic Kings...

Now, let's see Ferdinand Columbus' account:

... the Admiral went ashore with an armed boat, displaying the royal standard. The same was done by the captains of the other two ships, entering their boats with Spain's flag, in which a green cross was depicted, with an F on one side, and the other with other crowns in between D. Ferdinand and doña Isabel. After all of them were on their knees giving thanks to God, kissing the ground with tears of joy, the Admiral stood up and named the island San Salvador. Then he took possession of it in the name of the Catholic Kings with the proper ceremony and words, and in the presence of many of the natives of the island who came to see them. The Christians [the Spaniards] accepted him [Columbus] as Admiral, Viceroy, with pleasure and joy, and they swore him obedience as one who represented the royalty of our Majesties... (*Historia del Almirante,* Cap. XXII, pp. 102-103. Translation into English is mine. See *The Life of the Admiral Christopher Columbus* by his son Ferdinand, Ch. 23, p. 59).

In short, the primary historical sources, including "the first great historian," Bartolomé de las Casas, agreed that Columbus' first act after going ashore was indeed to give thanks to God for leading them safely across the sea.

Chapter 10. The Arrival

Howard Zinn's chapter on Columbus titled "Columbus, The Indians, and Human Progress" (from his *A People's History of the United States* book) is full of inaccuracies from the very first paragraph till the end of the chapter. Here is his first paragraph and what he claimed happened when Columbus came ashore on his first voyage:

> Arawak men and women, naked, tawny, and full of wonder, emerged from their villages onto the island's beaches and swam out to get a closer look at the strange big boat. **When** Columbus and his sailors came ashore, carrying swords, speaking oddly, **the Arawaks ran to greet them, brought them food, water, gifts**.

In other words, in his revisionist version, Zinn claimed the natives brought presents to Columbus, while Columbus, being the selfish "bully" that he was, gave nothing in return. However, that's not what happened. It was **Columbus**, and not the natives, **who gave gifts first**. Let's read what the actual account said:

> Soon many of the islanders gathered round us. I could see that they were people who would be more easily converted to our Holy Faith by love than by coercion, and wishing them to look on us with

friendship **I gave** some of them red bonnets and
glass beads which they hung round their necks, and
many other things of small value, at which they
were so delighted and so eager to please us that we
could not believe it. **Later** they swam out to the
boats to bring us parrots and balls of cotton thread
and darts, and many other things, exchanging them
for such objects as glass beads and hawk bells. They
took anything, and gave willingly whatever they had
(*Columbus' Journal, translated* by John Cummins,
Friday, October 12, 1492).

That doesn't sound like a "mean selfish bully." In another
paragraph Zinn said:

These Arawaks of the Bahama Islands were much
like Indians on the mainland, who were remarkable
(European observers were to say again and again)
for their hospitality, their belief in **sharing**. These
traits did not stand out in the Europe of the
Renaissance, dominated as it was by the religion of
popes, the government of kings, the frenzy for
money that marked **Western civilization** and its
first messenger to the Americas, Christopher Columbus.

I guess Columbus giving gifts and trading with the natives,
which he did in all four voyages as "the first messenger to the
Americas," doesn't count as "sharing"! Zinn added:

At one part of the island he [Columbus] got into a
fight with Indians who refused to trade as many
bows and arrows as **he** and his men wanted. Two
were run through with swords and bled to death.

The problem with that statement is that it is false. Columbus wasn't there, the fight was in self-defense, and the event took place three months later with a warlike tribe. This is more innuendo to keep portraying Columbus as a "selfish bully." This is what really happened:

> When the boat reached the shore a good fifty-five men were hiding in the trees... The Indian got out of the boat and made the others put down their bows and arrows and the heavy pieces of wood they were carrying instead of swords... They all came down to the boat, and the crew went ashore and began to buy the bows and arrows and other weapons, as I had told them to. After selling two bows the Indians refused to sell any more, but made as if to attack the crew and take them prisoner, running to pick up their bows and arrows from where they had left them and returning with ropes in their hands, apparently to tie up the men. The crew had their wits about them, for I always warn them to be on the alert for this, and when they saw the Indians running towards them they charged them, giving one of them a great sword-cut on the behind and shooting another in the chest with an arrow... When they came back in the boat to the ship and told me the story, I was partly saddened, but also pleased, for it is as well for these Indians to be afraid of us. The people here are clearly evilly disposed; I believe that these are the Caribs, and that they eat human flesh... If these are not the Caribs themselves, they must at least border with them, and their behaviour is the same... (*Columbus' Journal*, translated by John Cummins, Sunday, January 13, 1493).

More on the Caribs, or cannibals, later. On another subject, Zinn wrote:

> Las Casas describes sex relations: Marriage laws are non-existent men and women alike choose their mates and leave them as they please, without offense, jealousy or anger. They multiply in great abundance; pregnant women work to the last minute and give birth almost painlessly; up the next day, they bathe in the river and are as clean and healthy as before giving birth. If they tire of their men, they give themselves abortions with herbs that force stillbirths, covering their shameful parts with leaves or cotton cloth; although on the whole, Indian men and women look upon total nakedness with as much casualness as we look upon a man's head or at his hands.

Zinn failed to mention that the quote above is about a **specific** tribe; not all of them. Zinn also skipped the part where Las Casas said he did not believe the account, which came not from Las Casas himself, but from Amerigo Vespucci. This is what Las Casas wrote:

> Amerigo Vespucci relates all this in the account of his first voyage. I doubt that he understood so much in a few days he was there, especially since he admits to not having known the language -about the eight-year migrations for example, or the voluntary abortions by women tired of their men, or the absence of laws governing marriage and the ruling of the tribe (*History of the Indies* by Las Casas, Book Two, Ch. 164, pp. 64-65).

This is what Columbus said about natives and marriage:

As far as I have learned, every man throughout these islands is united to but one wife, with the exception of the kings and princes, who are allowed to have twenty (*Letter to Raphael Sanchez, May 1493*). [1]

In all the islands, as far as I could observe, the men are content with a single wife each, except that a chief or king has as many as twenty (*Letter to Luis de Santangel, March 4, 1493*). [2]

The reason why Amerigo Vespucci claimed that **specific** tribe didn't have "marriage laws," was because those natives sexually gave their women away to Amerigo and the Spaniards. They probably did that to keep the Spaniards as their allies, or maybe because that was their custom. [3] However, not every tribe was the same. In some places Columbus visited, husbands would hide their women out of jealousy, [4] while in others, women were celebrated because of their "chastity and grace." [5]

Chapter 11. They Would Make Fine Servants

"They were well-built, with good bodies and handsome features... They do not bear arms, and do not know them, for I showed them a sword, they took it by the edge and cut themselves out of ignorance. They have no iron. Their spears are made of cane... **They would make fine servants**... With fifty men we could subjugate them all and make them do whatever we want." [1]

The quote above is from Columbus' journal but edited by Howard Zinn and others as they saw fit to make it look like Columbus saw the natives as good candidates for slavery. The quote is one of the most popular memes on the Internet.

First of all, Columbus wasn't looking down on the Indians. Columbus was actually describing everything he saw, including the land, the trees, the streams, the people, as he arrived in the New World for the first time: "When we stepped ashore we saw fine green trees, streams everywhere and different kinds of fruit." Then Columbus described the natives physically:

> They go about as naked as the day they were born, even the women, though I saw only one, who was quite young. All the men I saw were quite young, none older than thirty, all well built, finely bodied and handsome in the face. Their hair is coarse, almost like a horse's tail, and short; they wear it

short, cut over the brow, except a few strands of hair hanging down uncut at the back. Some paint themselves with black, some with the colour of the Canary islanders, neither black nor white, others with white, others with red, others with whatever they can find. Some have only their face painted, others their whole body, others just their eyes or nose. They carry no weapons, and are ignorant of them; when I showed them some swords they took them by the blade and cut themselves. They have no iron; their darts are just sticks without an iron head, though some of them have a fish tooth or something else at the tip. They are all the same size, of good stature, dignified and well formed (*Columbus' Journal*, translated by John Cummins, Thursday, October 11, 1492).

Did you notice the difference between the Zinn quote, and the Columbus quote above, given its proper context? Columbus described the natives and praised them for their beauty, gentleness, and intelligence. He said, "They must be **good** servants, and **intelligent**, for I can see that they quickly repeat everything said to them. I believe they would readily become Christians." Funny how they skipped that last line.

Second, Columbus didn't say they "would **make** fine servants" or "fine slaves." What he said was that the natives "must **be** good servants." That's the way John Cummins, Samuel Eliot Morison, Hakluyt Society, and others translated it. But above all, that's what the original Spanish language says. [2] By the way, the natives had both slaves and servants too. Did you know that? Here is what Columbus said when he met the servant of a native chief:

The chief of this area, who has a village close to here, sent a large canoe to me full of his people, including one of his principal **servants**, to ask me to go in the ships to visit his land, where he would give me everything he had (*Columbus' Journal, translated* by John Cummins, Saturday, December 22, 1492).

We will discuss slavery in Chapter 22.

Third, the line, "with fifty men we could subjugate them," is not part of the same paragraph or context in Columbus' journal. That line was written three days later. Howard Zinn, and others, picked and chose the lines they wanted to give the impression Columbus was thinking about slavery from the first day he came ashore.

So, what does the line, "with fifty men we could subjugate them" mean? It means Columbus' assurance to the Queen of Spain (to whom his journal was addressed) that he could defeat the natives easily **IF** he had to fight them; especially since they had little knowledge on battle skills. The connotation here is one of conquest, and not of slavery. See Chapter 23.

In addition, revisionists won't mention that Columbus ended that first voyage in good terms with the natives. Another thing revisionists also fail to mention is that Queen Isabel was against slavery, especially enslaving Christians or Spanish subjects. So how can these verses mean Columbus wanted to enslave them, when he clearly stated, "they would readily become Christians," and Columbus saw them already as subjects of Spain?

They are the finest and gentlest folk in the world, and I trust in Our Lord God that Your Majesties will make Christians of them all, and that they will all be your people, which indeed I **now** hold them to be (*Columbus' Journal*, translated by John Cummins, Sunday, December 16, 1492).

Finally, primary historical source Bartolomé de las Casas, a man who was against slavery, was known as "the Apostle and defender of the natives" and sometimes was very critical of Columbus when it came to slavery, he didn't see Columbus' "fine servants" comment as one where Columbus was salivating over the natives as good candidates for slavery. That is remarkably interesting. In another place, Las Casas described a chief that he personally knew, as a "handsome" and a "well proportioned" person. Did that mean Las Casas wanted to enslave the native chief? Or was he just describing what the chief looked like? Las Casas also called Columbus, "an outstanding servant." Did that mean Las Casas wanted to enslave Columbus too? Or was he just praising Columbus, by using the same expressions Columbus used to praise the natives the first time he met them? I'm just asking. See *History of the Indies* by Las Casas, Book Two, Ch. 16, p. 118, and Book One, Ch. 80, p. 41.

Chapter 12. No King, No Religion

In order to give a utopian image of the natives, revisionists claim they didn't have a king or religion. James Loewen wrote: "Politically, nations like the Arawaks -without monarchs, without much hierarchy- stunned Europeans." [1]

Let's see what the primary historical sources have to say about the natives and their politics:

> When I [Columbus] saw that the **King** was on the beach, and that they were all paying him reverence, I sent him a gift which he accepted very ceremoniously. He is a young man of about twenty-one. He himself says little, having an old **tutor** and other **counsellors** who advise him and answer for him (*Columbus' Journal*, translated by John Cummins, Sunday, December 16, 1492).

> The **King** of this island of Española had risen early from his house some five leagues away, as I judge, and at the hour of terce he arrived in the village, which some of our company whom I had sent to see if any gold was arriving had already reached. They told me that more than two hundred men came with the **King**, and that four of them were carrying him on a litter (*Columbus' Journal*, translated by John Cummins, Tuesday, December 18, 1492).

When he [the King] came in under the sterncastle he made signs with his hands to tell all his people to stay outside, and they were very quick to obey him, sitting down on the deck; all except two elderly men whom I took to be his **tutor** and **counsellor**, who came and sat down at his feet (*Columbus' Journal*, translated by John Cummins, Tuesday, December 18, 1492).

I [Columbus] went ashore to eat, and arrived just after five **Kings** who are the **subjects** of the **King** here. His name is Guacanagarí. All five were wearing **crowns** to indicate their great authority. Your Majesties would have enjoyed seeing them; I believe **King** Guacanagarí must have ordered them to come to demonstrate his importance (*Columbus' Journal*, translated by John Cummins, Sunday, December 30, 1492).

This Isle of Hispaniola was made up of Six of their greatest **Kingdoms**, and as many most Puissant **Kings**, to whose **Empire** almost all the other **Lords**, whose Number was infinite, did pay their Allegiance... The **King** and **Lord** of this **Kingdom** was named Guarionex, who governed within the Compass of his **Dominions** so many **Vassals** and Potent **Lords**... [2]

In other words, the natives had kings, kingdoms, empires, dominions, crowns, lords, tutors, counselors, vassals, and subjects like anyone else.

About religion: If the natives didn't have religion, why would they lift their hands up in worship as Columbus arrived in the New World?

> The people kept coming down to the beach, calling to us and giving thanks to **God**. Some brought us water, some food; others, seeing that I did not wish to go ashore, swam out to us, and we understood them to be asking if we had come from **Heaven**. One old man climbed into the boat, and the others, men and women, kept shouting, 'Come and see the men who have come from **Heaven**; bring them food and drink.' Many men and women came, each bringing something and giving thanks to God, throwing themselves on the ground and raising their hands in the air (*Columbus' Journal*, translated by John Cummins, Sunday, October 14, 1492).

Earlier in this voyage, when Columbus said, "I can see from my own observations that these people have no religion, nor are they idolaters," he meant that he didn't see any temples or idols (*Columbus' Journal*, translated by John Cummins, Monday, November 12, 1492).

On another island, Columbus "found many statues in the shape of a woman and finely carved heads like masks," but he didn't "know if they" were "for decoration or worship" (*Columbus' Journal*, translated by John Cummins, Monday, October 29, 14-92).

A few years later, missionaries and others learned and told us what the natives' religious beliefs were. Ferdinand Columbus wrote about some of them, including their ceremonies, idol worship, mythologies, sorceries, drug induced rituals and the like, in Chapter 62 of his father's biography, *The Life of the Admiral Christopher Columbus.*

Among some of the religious beliefs that the natives had in common with some of us today are that they believed "that there is an immortal being in the sky whom none can see and who has a mother but no beginning" (*The Life of the Admiral Christopher Columbus* by his son Ferdinand, Ch. 62, p. 153).

Christopher Columbus met a native **cacique** (i.e. king or chief) who told him that "the souls of the good would go to **Heaven**, their bodies remaining on earth; but the souls of the wicked would go to **Hell**" (*The Life of the Admiral Christopher Columbus* by his son Ferdinand, Ch. 58, p. 141).

Primary historical source, Peter Martyr, also wrote about native religious beliefs in his book, *De Orbe Novo* (The First Decade, Book XI, pp. 167-175; The Second Decade, Book III, p. 219, and The Third Decade, Book I, p. 285).

> When the caciques wish to consult the zemes [i.e. idols] concerning the result of a war, about the harvest, or their health, they enter the houses sacred to them and there absorb the intoxicating herb called *kohobba*, which is the same as that used by the bovites to excite their frenzy. Almost immediately they believe they see the room turn upside down, and men walking with their heads downwards. This kohobba powder is so strong that those who take it lose consciousness; when the stupefying action of the powder begins to wane, the arms and hands become loose and the head droops (*De Orbe Novo* by Peter Martyr, The First Decade, Book IX, p. 174).

Can you imagine if that was Columbus instead of the natives? Revisionists would be adding a new accusation: "Columbus was drug addicted," a "drug lord," or "Columbus was a pimp!"

They also buried dead kings with their favorite wife alive:

> ... after the cacique dies the most beloved of his wives is buried with him. Anacaona, sister of Beuchios Anacauchoa, King of Xaragua, who was reputed to be talented in the composition of areytos, that is to say poems, caused to be buried alive with her brother the most beautiful of his wives or concubines, Guanahattabenecheua; and she would have buried others but for the intercession of a certain sandal-shod Franciscan friar, who happened to be present (*De Orbe Novo* by Peter Martyr, The Third Decade, Book IX, p. 387).

Where is the outrage against such fanaticism? Just imagine if that was Columbus and not the natives.

Jesuit missionaries also wrote about what the Brazilian natives believed, including the worship of thunder, the practice of witchcraft, cannibalistic rites, etc. And I haven't even mentioned the Aztecs, the Incas and the Maya civilization, who practiced human sacrifices, yet revisionists like to remind us of the Spanish Inquisition.

Some similar beliefs the Brazilian natives have with some of us today are that "they remember the Flood" and they claimed "that St. Thomas" visited there once (*History of the Indies* by Las Casas, Book One, Ch. 174, pp. 67-68).

I guess it's safe to say that the natives, whether in the islands or the Central and Southern mainland, did indeed have religious beliefs; some very different, some similar, but they did believe in religion and politics like anyone else back then.

Chapter 13. Racist

Some revisionists like to play the race card against Columbus. Maybe they haven't taken the time to read Columbus' own words concerning the natives. Columbus said the natives were *handsome, good looking, gentle, kind, generous, good-hearted, intelligent,* etc. (*The Voyage of Christopher Columbus*, Newly Restored and Translated by John Cummins, pp. 94, 95, 96, 100, 116, 137, 138, 141 and 148). That doesn't sound like a racist person at all.

> I swear to Your Majesties, I believe there can be no better people, nor a better land, anywhere on earth. They love their neighbors as themselves, and their speech is as gentle and kindly as can be, always with a smile. Men and women, it is true, go about as naked as they were born, but I assure Your Majesties that their behavior among themselves is above reproach (*Columbus' Journal*, translated by John Cummins, Tuesday, December 25, 1492).

That doesn't sound racist either. Revisionist James Loewen accused Columbus of racism. He wrote, "Columbus' own writings reflect this increasing racism. When Columbus was selling Queen Isabella on the wonders of the Americas, the Indians were 'well built' and 'of quick intelligence.' 'They have very good customs,' he wrote, 'and the King maintains a very marvelous state, of a style so orderly that it is a pleasure to see it, and they have good memories and they wish to see everything and ask what it is and for what it is used.' Later, when Columbus was justifying his wars and his enslavement of the Indians, they became '**cruel**' and 'stupid,' 'a people warlike and numerous, whose customs and religion are very different from ours.' " [1]

I don't know how describing someone as "warlike" makes anyone a racist. **The very first day** Columbus met the natives, he described them as "well built" and "of quick intelligence," but also "with scars," because "people from other islands nearby came to capture them." That is cruelty! Interesting how revisionists skipped that line! (*Columbus' Journal*, translated by John Cummins, Friday, October 12, 1492).

> We saw many fires in the night, and in the daytime many columns of smoke as if from watch towers. They appear to be on the alert, looking out for some people with whom they are at **war** (*Columbus' Journal*, translated by John Cummins, Thursday, December 6, 1492).

Also, the letter where Columbus complained against warlike natives, is the same letter where he complained against Spaniards, calling them "dissolute people who fear neither their King nor Queen," "full of imbecility," "malice," "hostile," "vagabonds," and "wicked." (*Writings of Christopher Columbus*, pp. 151-176).

Does that mean Columbus, a white man, was racist against other white men for using those kinds of adjectives? Mr. Loewen also said, "Columbus's son Ferdinand, who accompanied the admiral on his **third voyage**, reports that people they met or heard about in eastern Honduras 'are almost black in color, ugly in aspect,' probably Africans." [2]

First of all, Ferdinand Columbus accompanied Columbus on his FOURTH Voyage, not the third one. See *The Life of the Admiral Christopher* Columbus by his son Ferdinand, Ch. 88, p. 227.

Second, Columbus' son Ferdinand said they "were ugly" not because they looked "almost black," but because of their ASPECT, or appearance, instead. Here is the full sentence:

> But the people who live farther east, as far as Cape Gracias a Dios, are almost black in color, **ugly in aspect, wear no clothes, and are very wild in all respects. According to the Indian who was our prisoner, they eat human flesh** and raw fish, and pierce holes in their ears large enough to insert hen's eggs (*The Life of the Admiral Christopher Columbus* by his son Ferdinand, Ch. 90, p. 234).

In other words, not every tribe was the same. Some were kind, others more warlike, and others were "wild in all respects."

Third, Spaniards loved dark-skinned women. Where on earth does Mr. Loewen think we Hispanics came from!? Many Hispanics are a melting pot of European, Black, and native people! Since slavery and conflicts with the natives turned into a race issue in the United States, I think Mr. Loewen assumes that must be the case everywhere else.

Others have claimed Columbus misrepresented the natives by one day calling them "kind" and "generous," and later, "evil," "savage cannibals," "with dog-like noses that drink the blood of their victims." Benjamin Keen, translator of *The Life of the Admiral Christopher Columbus* wrote that "Many modern historians and anthropologists are skeptical of Columbus's ascription of cannibalism..." [3] This is evidence of how irresponsible, lazy and lousy are these so-called "scholars." Every primary source of the era, from the least, to the best, confirmed the acts of cannibalism, since many of them were witnesses to it, and/or some of their colleagues were victims of cannibalism as well. In addition, the natives' description of "evil" and rumors "that they eat people," came from the natives themselves, and not from Columbus. Up to that point, Columbus himself didn't believe that they ate anyone. Here is the actual quote in context:

> I also understood **them to say** that... to the S.E. ... there are men with one eye, and others with noses like dogs who eat human flesh; when they capture someone they cut his throat and drink his blood and cut off his private parts (*Columbus' Journal*, translated by John Cummins, Sunday, November 4, 1492).

> **The Indians** call it [an island] Bohio, and **say** it is very large inhabited by another people with one eye in their forehead, and others whom they call cannibals, of whom they are very afraid. When they saw that we were sailing on this course they could not speak; the people eat them, and are very well armed. I believe there is some truth in this, but if they are armed they must be people of intelligence. I think they must have taken some captives, and when they did not return it was probably thought that they had been eaten (*Columbus' Journal*, translated by John Cummins, Friday, November 23, 1492).

> All the people I have found so far are terrified of the 'Caniba' or 'Canima,' **who they say** live on the

island of Bohio, which must be very large. I believe they come to seize these people's land and houses because they are so cowardly and unskillful in fighting. I think these Indians whom we have on board live away from the coast because they are so close to this island of Bohio; when they saw me altering course for there they could not speak for fear that they were going to be eaten, and I could not reassure them. **They say** the Bohio people have faces like dogs and only one eye. I think they're lying; the people who take them captive must be under the rule of the Great Kahn (*Columbus' Journal*, translated by John Cummins, Monday, November 26, 1492).

The people of Cuba, or Juana, and all these other islands are very afraid of the people there, **for it is said** that they eat human flesh. **The Indians have told me** other remarkable things in sign language, **but I do not believe them.** The people of Bohio must simply be more intelligent and cunning in capturing them... (*Columbus' Journal*, translated by John Cummins, Wednesday, December 5, 1492).

The fact is that these islands, and many places in the American continent, were infected with cannibalism during this era. That is the reason why some of these natives were praising God; because they thought the Spaniards came from Heaven to save them from the Caribs, or cannibals. By the way, that is where the word "Caribe" (as in the Caribbean Sea) came from, which originated from the word "Carib," or "Caniba," in allusion of the cannibals. Should we rename the Caribbean Sea too?

To conclude, we can clearly see that Columbus was not a racist, and he didn't misrepresent the natives as some want us to think. Fake news. Nothing to see here.

Chapter 14. Shipwrecked

Two months after the discovery, the Santa María caravel ship-wrecked in Hispaniola (or La Española). Not long before that, Captain Pinzón had abandoned Columbus to seek gold by himself without authorization, leaving Columbus now with only one ship available.

Author and historian Laurence Bergreen accuses Columbus here of making "critical revisions" in his own journal about the shipwreck, by blaming the cause of the accident on the "inexperienced hand" of a young boy, but in another part, he placed the blame on the "treachery of the master and the people" for disobeying his orders. [1]

The fact is Columbus was talking about two different things: The **accident** was **caused** by the "inexperienced hand" of the young boy, **because** of the disobedience of the helmsman, but the ship couldn't be saved because of the disobedience of the master of the ship and "the people." That's what Columbus said. In other words, there are no contradictions or revisions here. Columbus wrote:

> I decided to lie down to sleep, for I had not slept for two days and a night. Seeing it was calm, the **helmsman** gave the helm to an apprentice seaman and went off to sleep. **I had strictly forbidden** the helm to be handed over to the apprentice seamen throughout the voyage, wind or no wind...

everyone lay down to sleep and the helm was left to the boy, and the currents took the ship very gently onto one of the banks, which could be heard and seen a good league away even at night. The boy, feeling the rudder grounding and hearing the noise of the sea, cried out, and I heard him and got up before anyone else had realized that we were aground. Then **the master**, who was officer of the watch, came on deck. I told him and **the others** to get into a boat we were towing, take an anchor and drop it astern. He jumped into the boat with a crowd of others, and I thought they were obeying my orders, but all they did was row off to the caravel half a league to windward (*Columbus' Journal,* translated by John Cummins, Tuesday, December 25, 1492).

It seems that the person making "critical revisions" here is Mr. Bergreen and not Columbus.

Chapter 15. Cannibals

Revisionists like to sweep the cannibal stories under the rug. They love to tell us about the Spaniards' brutality, but they look the other way when it comes to the cannibals. As we have seen, Columbus didn't believe the cannibal stories told by the natives, or at least that the Caribs were eating anyone. He just thought the Caribs were natives who were terrorizing their neighbors.

Columbus sent news to the local chief that his ship, the Santa María, had shipwrecked. The name of the chief was Guacanagarí. He was kind enough to help Columbus rescue the ship's cargo with his subjects. Because of that, Columbus promised Guacanagarí that he would get rid of the Caribs for him. That sounds like a hero. Don't you think? Here is the account:

> After our meal he [Guacanagarí] took me to the beach. I sent for a Turkish bow and a handful of arrows and ordered a good archer from among the ship's company to do some shooting. Not knowing about weapons, since they neither use nor possess them, the king was most impressed. This arose out of our conversation about the Caniba people, whom they call 'Caribs,' who come to capture them with bows and arrows. Their arrows are not tipped with iron. None of these lands seems to have any knowledge of iron or steel, or of any other metal except gold and copper; not that I have seen much

copper. I used sign language to tell the king that the King and Queen of Castile would send men to destroy the Caribs and hand them all over to him with their hands tied (*Columbus' Journal*, translated by John Cummins, Wednesday, December 26, 1492).

In addition to this, Columbus left 39 Spaniards in Hispaniola and returned to Spain. This way, he concluded his first voyage, without slavery, war or massacres. It was later, during Columbus' second voyage that he became convinced about cannibalism, as he was rescuing the "Taínos" [1] from the hands of the Caribs. This is what Peter Martyr said:

The Spaniards learned that there were other islands not far distant, inhabited by fierce peoples who live on human flesh; this explained why the natives of Hispaniola fled so promptly on their arrival. They told the Spaniards later that they had taken them for the cannibals, which is the name they give to these barbarians. They also call them *Caraibes*. The islands inhabited by these monsters lie towards the south, and about half-way to the other islands. The inhabitants of Hispaniola, who are a mild people, complained that they were exposed to **frequent attacks** from the cannibals who landed amongst them and pursued them through the forests like hunters chasing wild beasts. The cannibals captured children, whom they castrated, just as we do chickens and pigs we wish to fatten for the table, and when they were grown and become fat they ate them. Older persons, who fell into their power, were killed and cut into pieces for food; they also ate the intestines and the extremities, which they salted, just as we do hams. They did not eat women, as this would be considered a crime and an infamy. If they captured any women, they kept them and cared for them, in order that they might produce children; just as we do with hens, sheep, mares, and other animals. Old women, when captured, were made slaves (*De Orbe Novo* by Peter Martyr, The First Decade, Book I, pp. 62-63).

During Columbus' second voyage they found:

Birds were boiling in their pots, also geese mixed with bits of human flesh, while other parts of human bodies were fixed on spits, ready for roasting. Upon searching another house the Spaniards found arm and leg bones, which the cannibals carefully preserve for pointing their arrows; for they have no iron. All other bones, after the flesh is eaten, they throw aside. The Spaniards discovered the recently decapitated head of a young man still wet with blood (*De Orbe Novo* by Peter Martyr, The First Decade, Book II, p. 72).

Amongst other details given by the islanders on board, and as far as could be ascertained from their signs and their gestures, the cannibals of Montserrat frequently set out on hunts to take captives for food, and in so doing go a distance of more than a thousand miles from their coasts (*De Orbe Novo* by Peter Martyr, The First Decade, Book II, p. 74).

Most ferocious are those new anthropophagi, who live on human flesh, Caribs or cannibals as they are called. These cunning man-hunters think of nothing else than this occupation, and all the time not given to cultivating the fields they employ in wars and man-hunts. Licking their lips in anticipation of their desired prey, these men lie in wait for our compatriots, as the latter would for wild boar or deer they sought to trap (*De Orbe Novo* by Peter Martyr, The Third Decade, Book III, p. 315).

These atrocities kept happening even after Columbus' death. Here are some examples. Warning! Not for the weak or for the faint-hearted:

[In an expedition under Pedro Alonzo Nuñez] They encountered by chance a squadron of eighteen canoes full of cannibals engaged in a man-hunt: this was near the Boca de la Sierpe and the strait leading to the gulf of Paria, which I have before described. The cannibals unconcernedly approached the ship, surrounding it, and shooting flights of arrows and javelins at our men. The Spaniards replied by a cannon shot, which promptly scattered them. In pursuing them, the ship's boat came up with one of their canoes, but was able to capture only a single cannibal and a bound prisoner, the others having all escaped by swimming. This prisoner burst into tears, and by his gestures and rolling his eyes, gave it to be understood that six of his companions had been cruelly disembowelled, cut into pieces, and devoured by those monsters, and that the same fate awaited him on the morrow. They made him a present of the cannibal, upon whom he immediately threw himself, gnashing his teeth and belabouring him with blows of a stick and his fists and with kicks, for he believed that the death of his companions would not be sufficiently avenged till he beheld the cannibal insensible and beaten black and blue (*De Orbe Novo* by Peter Martyr, The First Decade, Book VIII, p. 155).

In the San Juan island, today known as Puerto Rico:

We have already said that the island of San Juan lies near to Hispaniola and is called by the natives Burichena. Now it is related that within our own time more than five thousand islanders have been carried off from Burichena for food, and were eaten by the inhabitants of these neighbouring islands which are now called Santa Cruz, Hayhay, Guadaloupe, and Quera queira. (*De Orbe Novo* by Peter Martyr, The Third Decade, Book V, p. 342).

In South America:

In these parts are found some of those abominable anthropophagi, Caribs, whom I have mentioned before. With fox-like astuteness these Caribs feigned amicable signs, but meanwhile prepared their stomachs for a succulent repast; and from their first glimpse of the strangers their mouths watered like tavern trenchermen. The unfortunate [Juan Diaz de] Solis landed with as many of his companions as he could crowd into the largest of the barques, and was treacherously set upon by a multitude of natives who killed him and his men with clubs in the presence of the remainder of his crew. Not a soul escaped; and after having killed and cut them in pieces on the shore, the natives prepared to eat them in full view of the Spaniards, who from their ships witnessed this horrible sight. Frightened by these atrocities, the men did not venture to land and execute vengeance for the murder of their leader and companions (*De Orbe Novo* by Peter Martyr, The Third Decade, Book X, pp. 401-402).

But Columbus was a horrible person. Right?

Chapter 16. What Revisionists Claim Happened

Columbus returned to Spain from his first voyage and was greeted as a hero. The Spanish monarchs immediately sponsored his next voyage in 1493; this time with 17 ships and 1,200 men with the intention to settle and work the Hispaniola island's gold mines. Revisionists complained that Columbus came *armed to the teeth*, ignoring that Europe (like the rest of the world) was at constant war with one another. He was "armed to the teeth" to protect the discoveries from future pirates and enemy countries; it wasn't intended to destroy the natives. In fact, Columbus was commanded by Queen Isabella to treat the natives "very well and lovingly," to give them presents from "Their Highness," and punish severely anyone who would mistreat them. [1]

It is on this second voyage that things went wrong. The following is what revisionists claim happened:

> When Columbus and his men returned to Haiti in 1493, they demanded food, gold, spun cotton - whatever the Indians had that they wanted, including sex with their women.

Wait a minute, I thought the natives didn't have marriage rules! I thought they would share everything, including the women! What happened to that one? The fictional account continues:

To ensure cooperation, Columbus used punishment by example. When an Indian committed even a minor offense, the Spanish cut off his ears or nose. Disfigured, the person was sent back to his village as living evidence of the brutality the Spaniards were capable of... After a while, the Indians had had enough... They refused to plant food for the Spanish to take... Finally, the Arawaks fought back. Their sticks and stones were no more effective against the armed and clothed... On March 24, 1495, he [Columbus] set out to conquer the Arawaks... Having as yet found no fields of gold, Columbus had to return some kind of dividend to Spain. In 1495 the Spanish on Haiti initiated a great slave raid. They rounded up 1,500 Arawaks, then selected the 500 best specimens (of whom 200 would die en route to Spain). Another 500 were chosen as slaves for the Spaniards staying on the island.

The quote above is from James Loewen and it's been repeated like gospel by everyone else in the media and the Internet. [2] Howard Zinn tells a similar imaginary version too:

Now, from his base on Haiti, Columbus sent expedition after expedition into the interior. They found no gold fields, but had to fill up the ships returning to Spain with some kind of dividend. In the year 1495, they went on a great slave raid, rounded up fifteen hundred Arawak men, women, and children, put them in pens guarded by Spaniards and dogs, then picked the five hundred best specimens to load onto ships. Of those five hundred, two hundred died en route. The rest arrived

91

alive in Spain and were put up for sale by the archdeacon of the town, who reported that, although the slaves were 'naked as the day they were born,' they showed 'no more embarrassment than animals.' Columbus later wrote: 'Let us in the name of the Holy Trinity go on sending all the slaves that can be sold.' [3]

The problem is that is not what happened.

Chapter 17. What Really Happened

As Columbus was on his way to Hispaniola, he explored the Caribbean while rescuing cannibal victims:

> Soon after the boats returned to pick up some Christians they had left in the land, they found with them six women who had fled from the Caribs and who came of their own will aboard the ships seeking protection. However, the Admiral not wishing to anger the people of that island, would not let them stay in the ships, and gave them some glass beads and hawk's bells and sent them back ashore.

Sounds like Columbus was considerate. Let's keep reading:

> ... which action was of no little prudence, because as soon as they set foot ashore, the Caribs stole what the Admiral gave them. Whereby, either because of hate or the fear they had of those Caribs, as soon as the boats returned for water and wood, these Indian women entered them, begging the sailors to take them aboard the ships, telling them with signs that the people of that island ate men and kept them as slaves and they did not wish to stay with them. In this way, the sailors were moved by their pleas and brought them back aboard the ships with two children and a young

man who had escaped the Caribs. They felt more secure with strangers from another nation and people they had never seen before than from those who without reserve were wicked cruel people who ate their sons and husbands (*Historia del Almirante,* Cap. XLVI, pp. 205-206. Translation into English is mine. See *The Life of the Admiral Christopher Columbus* by his son Ferdinand, Ch. 47, p. 113).

When Columbus reached Hispaniola, he found the 39 men he left there, from his first voyage, dead. A rival native chief named Caonabó, killed them all. Chief "Guacanagarí fought against Caonabó in defense of the Christians, but was wounded and fled" (*The Life of the Admiral Christopher Columbus* by his son Ferdinand, Chapters 49-50).

How did Columbus respond? He sailed to another part of the island and settled there. That doesn't sound like a "Hitler." In fact, according to Peter Martyr, "some persons advised Columbus to hold" Guacanagarí prisoner "to make him expiate in case it was proven that our compatriots had been assassinated by his orders; but the Admiral, deeming it inopportune to irritate the islanders, allowed him to depart" (*De Orbe Novo* by Peter Martyr, The First Decade, Book II, p. 80).

Do you think Hitler or Himmler would have done that? Dear reader, are you noticing how different the real Christopher Columbus is from the caricature made up by revisionists?

It was November 28th, 1493, when Columbus found his 39 men dead, but it wasn't until March 1494, that he decided "in order to show the Indians that they could not do to him what they had done to" the 39 men, "a large force stood ready to punish them if they molested a single" one of them (*The Life of the Admiral Christopher Columbus* by his son Ferdinand, Ch. 51, p. 123).

What did Columbus do next? Did he enslave the natives to work the gold mines? The answer is no. Columbus instead kept working the settlement, built forts for protection, stored food to eat, prepared to work the mines, built a dam, built a mill, etc., (*The Life of the Admiral Christopher Columbus* by his son Ferdinand, Ch. 53, p. 128).

In April, they found out that "Caonabó was preparing to march on the fort and burn it to the ground." Who was the aggressor again? See *The Life of the Admiral Christopher Columbus* by his son Ferdinand, Ch. 53, p. 127.

Columbus then sent Alonso de Hojeda with reinforcements to defend the fort, and apparently, Caonabó declined the attack. During this mission, Hojeda arrested a chief, his brother and one of his nephews, cutting the ear of one of them. The reason why was that some of them stole clothes from the Spaniards and their chief chose not to punish them. Cutting ears was the way theft was punished back then. Moreover, the chief kept the stolen clothes for himself and refused to return them back. When they brought these natives to Columbus, he decided to sentence them to death. Note that some Indigenous tribes punished some theft crimes with torture or death. In the meantime, another chief who came with them interceded for the lives of these men and Columbus forgave them (*The Life of the Admiral Christopher Columbus* by his son Ferdinand, Ch. 53, p. 129).

Do you think Hitler or Himmler would have forgiven anyone? I don't think so!

After Columbus set them free, a horseman reported that the natives of the village of the imprisoned chief captured five Spaniards and tried to kill them; but they were saved by the horseman who brought the news (*The Life of the Admiral Christopher Columbus* by his son Ferdinand, Ch. 53, p.129).

Someone might protest here that the theft committed by these natives was a petty one. But remember, Caonabó killed Columbus' 39 men from his first voyage; then killed more Spaniards later. He was also trying to unite more tribes to wipe out the rest of the Spaniards, as he did before, and now some natives were stealing without fear of consequences from their own leaders, thus losing respect for Columbus and his men.

Perhaps Columbus saw this as an opportunity to show the natives that he was resolute. That's the reason why, I believe, Columbus sentenced those natives to die, except that he ended up forgiving them instead. The reason why I said, "perhaps," or "I believe," is because Ferdinand Columbus, who usually explained his father's actions, didn't tell us why Columbus sentenced those natives to death. J.H. Langille's opinion on this event sounds plausible as well. He believed that "perhaps the execution was not intended to take place, but merely a sufficient scare of the poor savages to deter them from further theft." [1]

After Columbus forgave the natives, what did he do next? Genocide? Rape? Murder? Force them to work the mines? After all, that is what revisionists claim. Right? Remember, in their opinion, Columbus was a *Hitler* ... or *Himmler*. What did Columbus do next? He went to explore the islands and tried to find the continent.

Chapter 18. No Death or Destruction

On April 26th, 1494, Columbus "proceeded to the island of Tortuga..." No death or destruction.

On April 29th "he crossed over to Cuba." Natives brought food to Columbus "asking nothing in exchange. But the Admiral [Columbus], wishing to send them away happy, ordered them to be paid for everything..." No death or destruction.

May 3rd, Columbus "set sail from Cuba for Jamaica." In Jamaica, the Spaniards were attacked, so they wounded six or seven natives in self-defense. [1] After the "battle," a "multitude of canoes came **peacefully** from the neighboring villages to trade their things..." No death or destruction.

Later "that day... a young Indian came aboard saying he" wished "to go to Castile." His family begged him to come back, "but could not" turn "him from his design." Columbus "marveled at the firm resolution of this Indian and ordered him to be well treated." No death or destruction.

Columbus then went to Cuba. "As he had **never maltreated** the natives, the inhabitants, both men and women, gladly brought him gifts, displaying no fear." No death or destruction (*De Orbe Novo* by Peter Martyr, The First Decade, Book III, p. 101).

In Cuba, a cacique joined Columbus in a church mass on July 7th. No death or destruction.

On September 29th, Columbus ended the exploration. No death or destruction.

Except for the Peter Martyr quote above, the narrative and other quotes came from *The Life of the Admiral Christopher Columbus* by his son Ferdinand, Chapters 54 to 60.

Chapter 19. The Cutting of Hands

When Columbus came back from exploring Cuba and Jamaica, to Hispaniola, he found the island in revolt. The Spaniards in disobedience to Columbus' orders did not maintain the peace on the island, but instead went to steal and inflict injuries on the natives and their wives. Chief Guatiganá, along with other chiefs and their subjects, took revenge on the Spaniards by killing some of them. Columbus responded by arresting them, seizing some of their people and sent some of them as prisoners of war to Spain (*The Life of the Admiral Christopher Columbus* by his son Ferdinand, Ch. 61, pp. 147-148).

That's the event many revisionists have called the "slave raid," without providing any context of WHY Columbus sent some of them away as prisoners; without providing any context of why he told the Spaniards they could keep others for themselves. Yet Columbus let the rest of those he seized to go free. From these people Columbus let go free, some fled afraid they would be caught again, leaving "their infants anywhere on the ground." [1] Can you imagine if this was Columbus instead? Leaving his children behind as he fled from enemy combatants! Revisionists would be crying, "Columbus was a negligent father"!

All of this happened **almost one year later, around ten months after Columbus found his 39 men dead**! This is evidence of Columbus' patience, caution, and restraint. See *Historia de las Indias* by Las Casas, Tomo II, Lib. I, Cap. CII, p. 85.

You may wonder why Columbus punished the natives who killed the Spaniards and not the Spaniards who provoked the natives in the first place. The answer is that Guatiganá wasn't looking to stop the bloodshed. That's why Columbus intervened. Besides, some of the Spaniards were already punished by dying by the hands of the natives during this altercation, while others died of sickness. Most of those who survived returned to Spain. In addition, Columbus did indeed consistently punish the Spaniards for misbehavior.

Because of these events, Chief Caonabó now had the support of the other chiefs he was looking for, including Higuanamá, Behechio, and Guarionex, with the exception of Guacanagarí, to wipe out the Spaniards as he had done in the past. Chief Guacanagarí met with Columbus to let him know that he had no part in the schemes of the other chiefs. Behechio himself killed one of Guacanagarí's wives, while Caonabó kidnapped another one. Here Guacanagarí appealed to Columbus to save his wife and take revenge for the other. How is it possible that revisionists ignored all of this!? (*The Life of the Admiral Christopher Columbus* by his son Ferdinand, Ch. 61, p.148).

On March 24, 1495, (**one year and four months since the time Columbus found his 39 men dead**), Columbus marched forth in a warlike array, **with his ally Guacanagarí**, against Guatiganá, who had escaped custody, [2] and against the other chiefs, who gathered an army of more than one hundred thousand natives vs. Columbus' two hundred men, with their few horses and handful of dogs. Columbus fought them, defeated them, sold some as slaves and made the rest pay tribute. All these things were the normal customs during war back then.

The natives **promised** Columbus they would pay the tribute, which is another thing revisionists won't mention. The reason why I say this is, if this was Columbus, making a promise, and then not keeping it, revisionists would be having a fit.

This pact suited both parties," said Peter Martyr. The tribute consisted of those who **lived where the gold mines were**, fourteen years of age and up, were to pay a large hawk's bell of gold dust (*De Orbe Novo* by Peter Martyr, First Decade Book IV, p. 111).

In Chapter 52 of *The Life of the Admiral,* natives were already giving away some of the gold dust as presents to the Spaniards. That might be the reason why Columbus asked for it as a tribute. In other words, Columbus asked what he thought, at that moment, the natives could give. All others were to pay twenty-five pounds of cotton.

> Whenever an Indian delivered his tribute, he was to receive a brass or copper token which he must wear about his neck as proof that he had made his payment; any Indian found without such a token was to be punished (*The Life of the Admiral Christopher Columbus* by his son Ferdinand, Ch. 61, p. 150).

That's where revisionists swear the punishment for not paying tribute was to cut off their hands. The problem with this assumption is that primary sources like Ferdinand Columbus and Peter Martyr didn't specify the punishment. Bartolomé de las Casas, the defender of the natives, said that the unnamed punishment was a moderate one (*Historia de las Indias* by Las Casas, Tomo II, Lib. I, Cap. CV, p. 102).

If the punishment was to cut off the natives' hands, Las Casas wouldn't call it "moderate."

Antonio de Herrera added that because it was hard for the natives to bring such tribute, which caused many of them to flee to the mountains, Columbus decided to cut the hawk bell quota in half. That is another detail revisionists will avoid telling you

(*Historia General* by Herrera, Década I, Lib. II, Cap. XVII, p. 61. Also *Historia de las Indias* by Las Casas, Tomo II, Lib. I, Cap. CV, p. 104).

So, when revisionists quote, "they would cut an Indian's hand and leave them dangling by a shred of skin," they are actually jumping timelines, either purposely, or just by ignorance. They are quoting events that took place years after Columbus was out of office, and the actions were committed by corrupt Spaniards during the governance of "El Comendador de Lares," Nicolás de Ovando. In other words, they are blaming Columbus for things he didn't commit, or things that happened when he was not around, by the actions of worthless men who were acting on their own, against the policies of the Queen of Spain and Christopher Columbus. See *History of the Indies* by Las Casas, Book Two, Ch. 8, p. 94, and Ch. 15, p. 118.

Chapter 20. Diseases, Starvation, and Death

Another ridiculous accusation against Columbus is that he brought sickness and diseases as if they didn't exist in the New World before 1492. More sickening is that some schools teach this garbage to little children. The fact is, sickness and disease existed before, during, and after Columbus, in both the Old and the New World.

Some people want to blame Columbus for bringing syphilis to the New World, even though he personally wasn't "sleeping around" with anyone. Ridiculous! Incidentally, the natives experienced syphilis before 1492. It's even in their own mythologies, as recorded by Ferdinand Columbus in *The Life of the Admiral Christopher Columbus,* Ch. 62, page 155.

When talking about death, revisionists like to point out that a third of the population Hispaniola died from 1494 to 1496, without providing any context. Let's continue the story, where we left, and see what happened. Columbus defeated the natives of Hispaniola in war and eventually he captured Caonabó:

> After the capture of Caonabo and all his household, the Admiral resolved to march throughout the whole island. He was informed that the natives suffered from such a severe famine that more than 50,000 men had already perished, and that people continued to die daily as do cattle in time of pest.

This calamity was the consequence of their own folly; for when they saw that the Spaniards wished to settle in their island, they thought they might expel them by creating a scarcity of food. They, therefore, decided not only to plant no more crops, but also to destroy and tear up all the various kinds of cereals used for bread which had already been sown... (*De Orbe Novo* by Peter Martyr, The First Decade, Book IV p. 108).

That's the context of WHY many natives died during Columbus' second voyage. Some people want to add the number of people who died of illnesses or the handful of wars that happened afterwards (*Historia de las Indias* by Las Casas, Tomo II, Libro I, Cap. CVI, p. 106).

Revisionists failed to mention that some of those wars were Indigenous tribes fighting each other with the assistance or at the request of Columbus or his brothers.

On the subject of "depopulation," did you know natives were depopulating one another long before Columbus arrived? "At the island of Monserrate... [Columbus] learned from the Indians aboard that the Caribs had **depopulated** that island by eating **all** its inhabitants (*The Life of the Admiral Christopher Columbus* by his son Ferdinand, Ch. 48, p. 116).

Where are the revisionists protesting this kind of injustice and depopulation caused by other natives?

As stated before, Columbus sold some of the defeated combat enemies to Spain as slaves. Revisionists love to remind us that many of them died on their way there, as if that was part of the plan, or something that Columbus would rejoice about. In the first place, Columbus wasn't the captain of that ship. Secondly, the natives probably died for the same reasons Spaniards died too; "because of the unaccustomed air," which in the case of

Spain, was "colder than theirs." [1] This is also the reason why Columbus later said in a letter that, "although they die now, they will not always die." (*Historia de las Indias* by Las Casas, Tomo II, Lib. I, Cap. CLI, p. 324). Las Casas clarified here that Columbus wrote that statement in broken Spanish, as an Italian man whose Spanish was "defective." The reason why I mentioned this point is because some revisionists are using this ill-written statement, as proof that Columbus didn't care about anyone, not even slaves, and "viewed the Indian death rate optimistically." [2] In addition, he was a racist pig, because he said in the next sentence that, "the **Negroes** and Canary Islanders died at first."

Maybe revisionists don't know that the word **Negro** in Spanish is not a racial slur, like it is today in the English language in North America. "Negro" means black, or a black person. What Columbus really meant with the statement above was that he expected the native slaves to live, and not to die, like it happened the first time they sent them to Spain. It's incredible what context can do!

Now, did you know that many Spaniards got sick and died too? Why do revisionists fail to mention this? Why do you think Columbus had only 200 men to fight 100,000 natives, when he came with 1,200 Spaniards on his second voyage? The reason is, because most of them got sick due to "the climate and diet of that country," others died, and many returned back to Spain (*The Life of the Admiral Christopher Columbus* by his son Ferdinand, Ch. 51, p. 122).

Any sympathy here?

Because of these miseries, it was reported that some Spaniards saw ghosts and others heard terrifying voices in the day and in the night in the town of Isabela. Eventually, Isabella town was abandoned and the people wouldn't dare to walk close by (*History of the Indies* by Las Casas, Book One, Ch. 92, p. 50).

In the meantime, Columbus returned to Spain to bring more supplies and left his brothers, Bartholomew and Diego, in charge of Hispaniola. Peter Martyr wrote that during that time, "About three hundred of his [Spanish] men had fallen victims to divers maladies, and he [Bartholomew Columbus] was therefore much concerned and hardly knew what course to adopt, for everything was lacking, not only for caring for the sick, but also for the necessities of life" (*De Orbe Novo* by Peter Martyr, The First Decade, Book V, p. 120).

After Columbus was out of office, Spaniards were still suffering. Las Casas said that "they caught fever from the climate, which was aggravated by the lack of food, of care and shelter; and they died at such a rate the priest barely managed to bury them. Out of 2,500 men, more than 1,000 died, while 500 cases of illness were made worse by anguish, hunger and need; and from then on, this was the lot of whoever came to the New World to find gold" (*History of the Indies* by Las Casas, Book Two, Ch. 6, p. 88).

Anyone lamenting this?

Many times, Columbus himself suffered sickness, hunger, or lived on low rations of food (*The Life of the Admiral Christopher Columbus* by his son Ferdinand, Ch. 59, p. 142).

At one time, "he had a high fever and a drowsiness, so that he lost his sight, memory, and all his other senses" (*The Life of the Admiral Christopher Columbus* by his son Ferdinand, Ch. 60, p. 145).

During his second voyage, Columbus was "suffering so acutely from arthritis that he kept his bed for weeks on end..." [3]

During Columbus' third voyage, Ferdinand Columbus stated "that his father suffered from inflamed eyes, and that from about" that "time he was forced to rely for information upon his sailors and pilots" (*De Orbe Novo* by Peter Martyr, The First Decade, Book VI, p. 135, Footnote 2).

Why are revisionists only "concerned" when the natives got sick and died, and not when the Spaniards and Columbus suffered the same fate? Why don't they even bother to mention it? Why do they pick and choose who they want us to feel sorry for?

Chapter 21. Gold and Greed

Howard Zinn wrote: "Now, from his base on Haiti [Hispaniola] Columbus sent expedition after expedition into the interior. They found no gold fields..." [1] That statement is false. The fact is that there was gold, among other things. Ferdinand Columbus said that there were "many rivers containing gold... high mountains in whose streams they found gold dust... mines and river sands abound in gold" (*The Life of the Admiral Christopher Columbus* by his son Ferdinand, Ch. 52, p. 126).

> Moreover, they had daily new confirmation of the wealth of the island; for not a day passed without the return of one of the men the Admiral had dispatched in different directions with news of the discovery of new mines, not to mention the accounts brought by the Indians of the discovery of great quantities of gold in various parts of the island (*The Life of the Admiral Christopher Columbus* by his son Ferdinand, Ch. 54, p. 131).

In addition, "much was learned about the resources and secrets of the land: that it had mines of copper, sapphires, and amber; brazilwood, ebony, incense, cedars, many fine gums, and different kinds of wild spices..." (*The Life of the Admiral Christopher Columbus* by his son Ferdinand, Ch. 62, pp. 150-151).

Since Columbus was always underestimated, he sarcastically wrote a letter in 1500 saying that "much gold is being exploited today that opinion is divided as to what is more profitable: to steal or to work the mines" (*History of the Indies* by Las Casas, Book One, Ch. 181, p. 73).

Las Casas later reported that when Columbus was dying, "the reputation of the wealth of the Indies was spreading like wildfire and brought great quantities of gold to Castile" (*History of the Indies* by Las Casas, Book Two, Ch. 38, p. 143).

What was the problem then? The problem was that many Spaniards came to America thinking they would get rich quick. They "did not know that gold may never be had without the sacrifice of time, toil, and privations," said Ferdinand Columbus. "As matters did not turn out as they expected, and they were disgruntled at having to work on the construction of the new town," and many of them gave up and left (*The Life of the Admiral Christopher Columbus* by his son Ferdinand, Ch. 51, p. 122).

Like Las Casas said, "gold does not grow on trees" (*History of the Indies* by Las Casas, Book One, Ch. 107, p. 56, and Book Two, Ch. 6, p. 88).

Peter Martyr wrote, "It is a fact that the people who accompanied the Admiral in his second voyage were for the most part undisciplined, unscrupulous vagabonds, who only employed their ingenuity in gratifying their appetites" (*De Orbe Novo,* The First Decade, Book IV, p. 106).

Meanwhile, two important Spanish men, Pedro Margarit and Friar Boyl, "departed for Spain animated by evil intentions." They were not happy with how things turned out in Hispaniola.

> In order that he [Columbus] might justify himself before the sovereigns, in case they should have been prejudiced by the reports of his enemies, and also for the purpose of recruiting colonists to replace those who had left, and to replenish the failing

foodstuffs, such as wheat, wine, oil, and other provisions which form the ordinary food of Spaniards, who do not easily accustom themselves to that of the natives, he decided to betake himself to the Court... (*De Orbe Novo* by Peter Martyr, The First Decade, Book IV, p. 105).

'If the Spaniards have brought several shiploads of scarlet wood and some gold, and a little cotton and some bits of amber back to Europe, why did they not load themselves with gold and all the precious products which seem to abound so plenteously in the country you describe?' Columbus answered such questions by saying that the men he had taken with him thought more of sleeping and taking their ease than about work, and they preferred fighting and rebellion to peace and tranquility. The greater part of these men deserted him (*De Orbe Novo* by Peter Martyr, The First Decade, Book IV, p. 110).

In other words, there was gold, but the Spaniards either didn't want to work, or they were too sick to work. That's the reason why there was no immediate return of wealth during this second voyage.

Revisionists charge Columbus as greedy because he was searching for gold, as if getting paid for one's work would define someone as greedy. Columbus' job was for profit, and not for charity; not to mention that he had a lot of expenses before he made any profit. Further, his job was full of constant danger, including hurricanes, storms, waterspouts, shipwrecks; that's without counting sickness, hunger, mutinies, revolts, political coups, battles, etc. What's wrong with getting paid for one's job?

To prove Columbus was greedy, revisionists like to quote the following statement made by him during his third voyage, as evidence:

> Gold is the most precious of all commodities; gold constitutes treasure, and he who possesses it has all he needs in this world, as also the means of rescuing souls from purgatory, and restoring them to the enjoyment of paradise (*Writings of Christopher Columbus*, p. 230).

Gold is precious and constitutes treasure, indeed. I don't know what's wrong with that statement. The second part of the quote is about Columbus expressing the mystic beliefs of his day. The irony is that revisionists skipped the next sentence, which says that, "they [the natives] say that when one of the lords of the country of Veragua dies, they bury all the gold he possessed with his body." These natives were to abstain from food and from "the company of their wives" as they collected gold from "far off rugged mountains" (*The Life of the Admiral Christopher Columbus* by his son Ferdinand, Ch. 94, p. 250).

Washington Irving commented that a "superstitious notion with respect to gold appears to have been very prevalent among the natives. The Indians of Hispaniola observed the same privations when they sought for it; abstaining from food and from sexual intercourse. Columbus, who seemed to look upon gold as one of the sacred and mystic treasures of the earth, wished to encourage similar observances among the Spaniards; exhorting them to purify themselves for the researches among the mines by fasting, prayer, and chastity. It is scarcely necessary to add, that his advice was but little attended to by his rapacious and sensual followers." [2]

If Columbus was greedy because of his mysticism about gold, would it be fair to say the same about the natives, who also had their share of mysticism about gold too? I'm not being critical of the natives on this point; I'm just showing the reader the double standard and dishonesty from revisionists toward Columbus.

Chapter 22. Slavery, the Unpardonable Sin

Slavery is revisionists' favorite subject. They want to stigmatize Columbus with slavery, as if slavery was invented by Columbus, or that it was something new back then. Perhaps they don't know that slavery existed before, during and after Columbus, and was a common practice throughout history. Las Casas' biographer, Francis Augustus MacNutt wrote:

> The records of the earliest peoples of whom history preserves knowledge —Chaldeans, Egyptians, Phoenicians, and Arabians— show that slavery has existed from the remotest antiquity. Slavery was the common fate of prisoners of war in the time of Homer; Alexander sold the inhabitants of Thebes, and the Spartans reduced the entire population of Helos to servitude, so that Helot came to be synonymous with slave, while one of the laws inscribed on the Twelve Tables of Rome gave a creditor the right to sell an insolvent debtor into slavery to satisfy his claim. Wealthy Romans frequently possessed thousands of slaves, over whose lives and fortunes the owners were absolute masters. [1]

Columbus is the most unfairly treated historical figure. Revisionists want us to remember Columbus for slavery and not for his discoveries. They want us to associate Columbus with slavery, like we associate abolishment of slavery with Abraham Lincoln today. That's not fair. Do we think of slavery when we talk about Plato, Cicero, Marco Polo, or George Washington? Of course not, even though they owned slaves!

They tell us Columbus' legacy is one of slavery. My question is: If Columbus' legacy is slavery, then, why don't we practice it today? The reason is because Columbus' legacy is NOT slavery. Columbus' legacy was the import of Christianity and the ideas of Western civilization, which three centuries later abolished the slavery revisionists complain about. Before Columbus, slavery was practiced for thousands of years in both the Old and the New World. After Columbus' death, slavery was abolished, in the New World, three hundred and fifty-nine years later.

If Columbus was really thinking about slavery from the very first time he landed, as some revisionists claim, then why didn't he enslave them right then and there? Why did he call them "kind" and "generous" people? Why didn't he call them "evil" instead, even if it was a lie? That could have given him a reason to enslave them immediately.

Why did he bring the Spaniards to work the gold mines on his second voyage if he was planning to enslave the natives anyway? Why didn't Columbus enslave them as soon as he found his 39 men dead during his second voyage? After he defeated the natives, in war, why did he still request Spain to bring more Spaniards to work the gold mines during his third voyage? [2]

The other thing is the cleverness of the word "slavery" used by revisionists. What do people think when they hear that word? Probably, innocent people kidnapped and sold as slaves for no reason whatsoever, like they used to do with the African slave trade. The problem is that the Queen of Spain was against the enslavement of the natives, something revisionists won't tell you. Later, she reluctantly allowed Columbus to enslave only native

enemy combatants or criminals for a period of time as he was forced to fight some of the tribes in Hispaniola. That's another detail skipped by revisionists. [3]

So, there you have the so-called "slaves" Columbus sent to Spain. That is, the cannibals he took prisoners as promised to Chief Guacanagarí, and the enemies he defeated in war on Hispaniola in 1495.

By the way, getting rid of the cannibals was something that pleased the natives around the Caribbean! However, the problem with enslaving a conquered nation, back then in Columbus' times, was that noncombatant persons, including women and children, were also fair candidates for slavery. That's what makes slavery in Columbus' time, so upsetting. Thank God, we don't practice slavery anymore!

Columbus then sent the very first slaves to the queen with the following suggestions:

> ... we have no interpreter through whom we can make these people acquainted with our holy faith, as their Highnesses and we ourselves desire, and as we will do so soon as we are able, we send by these two vessels some of these **cannibal** men and women, as well as some children, both male, and female, whom their Highnesses might order to be placed under the care of the most competent persons to teach them the language.

Notice he didn't ask to put them under the whip, but under "competent persons to teach them the language." He continued:

> At the same time they might be employed in useful occupations, and by degrees through somewhat **more care** being bestowed upon them **than** upon

other slaves, they would learn one from the other...
But as amongst all these islands, those inhabited by
the cannibals are the largest and the most populous,
it must be evident that nothing but good can come
from sending to Spain men and women who may
thus one day be led to abandon their barbarous
custom of eating their fellow-creatures. By learning
the Spanish language in Spain, <u>they will much
earlier receive baptism</u> and advance the welfare of
their souls...

Note: If Columbus was looking for their baptism, or for
them to become Christians, then this is another piece of evidence
that the slavery he was proposing was temporary, since enslaving
Christians was against Spanish law.

...moreover, we shall gain great credit with the
Indians who do not practice the above-mentioned
cruel custom, when they see that we have seized and
led captive those who injure them, and whose very
name alone fills them with horror... when they see
the **good treatment** that we shall shew to those
who do well, and the punishment that we shall
inflict on those who do wrong, will hasten to
submit, so that we shall be able to lay our com-
mands on them as vassals of their Highnesses...
(*Memorial Letter to Antonio de Torres by Columbus,* from *Select Letters of Christopher Columbus,*
pp. 85-86).

Some revisionists contend that this *Memorial Letter*
proves Columbus' intention of enslaving the natives from the very
beginning. All because he used the word "intelligent," to describe

the natives, as he did in his journal. This is quite a stretch. Columbus was talking about the cannibals here, and not the Taínos. "Well-proportioned and very intelligent" were the only compliments Columbus gave these cannibals because next he described them as "savages" and "cruel," which in reality, they were. Columbus was looking to enslave the cannibals; not the Taínos. Remember, he promised the natives, he would get rid of the cannibals for them. That's why he suggested in this letter to capture more of them, and use them as slaves, but with the expectation that they will abandon "the cruel habits to which they have become accustomed," and "forget their cruel customs," once "they are out of their country."

Years later, in a memorandum, Columbus confirmed again that he "intended to reclaim" the natives "and return them to their lands so they would instruct others" (*History of the Indies* by Las Casas, Book Two, Ch. 37, p. 141).

For the ignorant cynic, there is no winning argument here. Columbus loses no matter what he has done. If Columbus had killed the cannibals, he would be *bad*. If he had not done anything about it, he would've been *bad* for not caring for the peaceful natives who were their victims. If he had captured and sold them as slaves, as he did, he would be *bad* anyway for trying to make a "quick buck." If he had called the natives "ugly," he would be *racist*, but if he called them "handsome," that meant he wanted to enslave them.

During Columbus' third voyage, there was an instant where the queen indignantly exclaimed, "what power has the admiral" Columbus "to give away my vassals?" as more slaves arrived in Spain from Hispaniola, at a time when Spaniards were slandering Columbus, and Francisco Roldán was leading a rebellion against him. The queen didn't know what was true or false at that moment. The irony here is that she was the one who sanctioned the slavery. However, the queen set those slaves free.

The slaves Columbus sent at that time, were sent because of the capitulations he was **forced** to sign during Roldán's rebellion. More on the rebellion in Chapter 25. Las Casas explained that during the rebellion, Columbus "assigned a tribe of Indians to Francisco Roldán and a few others to do work for them or find gold" (*History of the Indies* by Las Casas, Book Two, Ch. 1, p. 79).

Columbus gave the rebels everything they demanded, while at the same time, he was sending secret letters to Spain asking for help and reporting the violent abuses the Spaniards were inflicting onto the natives. Those slaves were demanded by Roldán, and Columbus willingly sent them to Spain so the queen could see the chief's daughters pregnant, giving her a hint of what Roldán and his accomplices were doing to the natives. The queen was upset because she did not know what troubles Columbus was suffering at that moment and his letters did not reach her on time. That's the context of the queen's indignant outcry episode (*Historia General* by Herrera, Década I, Lib. III, Cap. XVI, pp. 93-95; Lib. IV, Cap. VII, pp. 108-110, and *Historia de las Indias* by Las Casas, Tomo II, Lib. I, Cap. CLIX, p. 360).

Another point I want to emphasize here is that from all the places Columbus visited in the Caribbean, Central and South America, he only enslaved the natives of Hispaniola, some cannibals who were terrorizing the islands, and a chief (along with some hostages) who had intended to assassinate him in the mainland during his fourth voyage. In other words, Columbus wasn't enslaving the natives of every place he visited, as revisionists want us to think. He didn't enslave, for example, the people of Cuba, Puerto Rico, Dominica, Jamaica, Trinidad, Honduras, Nicaragua, Panamá, etc. He only enslaved those he defeated in war or self-defense, and as a last resort.

Some revisionists claim Columbus started the transatlantic slave trade, which is not true. The transatlantic slave trade was started by the Portuguese after Columbus was dead, bringing African slaves to the New World. Other revisionists modify their assertion by claiming Columbus transported native slaves to Spain, crossing the Atlantic, which counts as a "transatlantic slave trade." They ignore that the natives practiced slavery too, and in the case of the Caribs, they used to cross the Atlantic Ocean to terrorize and enslave the Taino women in the islands. That is an Atlantic slave trade, or slave raid long before 1492. Decades later, after Columbus was dead, the natives would make peace treaties with the Spaniards and would guide them to their native enemies so the Spaniards would enslave them for them. [4]

But, what about the Taínos?

Peter Martyr wrote that before Caonabó was arrested, "several caciques... urge [him] not to allow the Christians to settle in the island, unless he wished to exchange independence for **slavery**" (*De Orbe Novo* by Peter Martyr, The First Decade, Book IV, p. 107).

How did the Taínos of Hispaniola come to this idea of slavery if they were strangers to the concept?

During Columbus' fourth voyage, he visited the island of Guanaja, off the coast of Honduras. Peter Martyr wrote:

This island is incredibly fertile and luxuriant. While coasting along its shores, the Admiral [Columbus] met two of those barques dug out of tree trunks of which I have spoken. They were drawn by naked **slaves** with ropes round their necks. The chieftain of the island, who, together with his wife and children, were all naked, travelled in these barques. When the Spaniards went on shore the **slaves**, in obedience to their master's orders, made them understand by haughty gestures that they would have to obey the chief, and when they refused, menaces and threats were employed (*De Orbe Novo* by Peter Martyr, The Third Decade, Book IV, p. 317).

Subsequent explorers testified of the practice of slavery by the natives. For example, Vasco Núñez de Balboa explored some places in South America where he met one of the sons of a chief. This is what Martyr wrote about:

> The eldest of the seven sons of Comogre was a young man of extraordinary intelligence... He therefore presented four thousand drachmas of wrought gold and seventy **slaves** to Vasco Nuñez and Colmenares, as they were the leaders (*De Orbe Novo* by Peter Martyr, The Second Decade, Book III, p. 220).

> The son of Comogre... spoke again as follows, ... 'Here is one of our servants who was once the **slave** of the cacique who possesses such treasures of gold, and is the ruler beyond the mountains; there this man dragged out several years of a wretched existence' (*De Orbe Novo* by Peter Martyr, The Second Decade, Book III, p. 222).

Martyr also tells us of a group of blacks who were living close to Quarequa, Panamá. It seems that they were either black pirates from Ethiopia, whose vessel shipwrecked, or black slaves carried by those pirates, or maybe a combination of both, but they were described as "fierce and cruel." He added:

> The natives of Quarequa carry on incessant war with these negroes. Massacre or **slavery** is the al-

ternate fortune of the two peoples (*De Orbe Novo* by Peter Martyr, The Third Decade, Book I, p. 286).

[In another place] When the Spaniards [under Vasco's leadership] left his village he [Chief Taocha] not only furnished them guides, but also **slaves** who were prisoners of war and who took the place of beasts of burden in carrying on their shoulders provisions for the march (*De Orbe Novo* by Peter Martyr, The Third Decade, Book II, p. 298).

Some of these tribes were described as "their only object being to murder or to **enslave** one another in their warlike incursions" (*De Orbe Novo* by Peter Martyr, The Third Decade, Book III, p. 305).

Vasco met another chief where they traded with each other. Vasco "gave [Chief] Pochorroso the usual acceptable articles, and the cacique gave Vasco fifteen pounds of melted gold and some **slaves** (*De Orbe Novo* by Peter Martyr, The Third Decade, Book III, p. 308).

In 1515 Conquistador Gonzalo de Badajoz went to a village where "They found, however, some **slaves** who were branded in a painful fashion. The natives cut lines in the faces of the **slaves**, using a sharp point either of gold or of a thorn; they then fill the wounds with a kind of powder dampened with black or red juice, which forms an indelible dye and never disappears" (*De Orbe Novo* by Peter Martyr, The Third Decade, Book X, p. 404).

And I haven't mentioned the horrible things the Mayas, Incas and Aztecs used to do to their slaves! Any outrage about these? Should we stigmatize the natives with slavery, too? Should we still celebrate Indigenous Peoples' Day? If slavery makes Columbus "evil," should we say the same about the natives? Or, is this just another example of selective moral outrage?

Chapter 23. Conquest

Revisionists are flabbergasted by the idea of conquest in regard to Columbus. This is another subject revisionists treat as something new or something Columbus invented, but the reality is the same way war and slavery existed before, during, and after Columbus, so it was with conquest. It was also practiced by everyone back then, including the natives.

Some people live as if history started the day they were born, but history existed before we were born. Life was very different in the past than it is today in the present. For example, in Columbus' day, politics were very different. Presidents weren't elected every four years by the people. Instead, they had kings, kingdoms, empires, and the practice of conquest. I don't know why this seems to be a foreign concept to modern "scholars." I don't know why people would expect Columbus to behave differently in a time where conquest was the rule of the day. Columbus was doing what everyone else had been doing for thousands of years before him.

Columbus saw himself as a conqueror as well. He said:

> I ought to be judged as a captain sent from Spain to the Indies, to **conquer** a nation numerous and warlike, with customs and religion altogether different to ours; a people who dwell in the mountains, without regular habitations for themselves or for us; and where, by the Divine will, I have sub-

dued another world to the dominion of the King and Queen, our Sovereigns; in consequence of which, Spain, that used to be called poor, is now the most wealthy of kingdoms (*Writings of Christopher Columbus*, p. 171).

That's why I stated earlier that "with fifty men we could subjugate them all and make them do whatever we want," was a statement of conquest and not slavery. The statement was addressed to the Queen of Spain, who was against slavery, but fine with conquest. The King and the Queen of Spain entitled Columbus as Don, admiral, viceroy, and governor of the islands and the mainland he discovered. That's evidence they were aiming at conquest from the beginning. See *The Life of the Admiral Christopher Columbus* by his son Ferdinand, Ch. 44, pp. 103-108.

I'm surprised revisionists didn't exploit the following quote as "evidence" of Columbus "intentions" to enslave the natives: "three men could put a thousand of them to flight, so they could easily be commanded and made to work, to sow and to do whatever might be needed to build towns and be taught to wear clothes and adopt our ways" (*Columbus' Journal*, translated by John Cummins, Sunday, December 16, 1492).

The problem, of course, is that if you read a few lines up, Columbus is talking to the queen, telling her:

Rest assured that this island and all the others are as firmly in **your** possession as Castile; we only have to establish ourselves and order the people to do whatever **you** [the queen] wish (*Columbus' Journal*, translated by John Cummins, Sunday, December 16, 1492).

It's fascinating to see how loyal a man Columbus was to the crown, even though he was not a Spaniard. Columbus was trying to impress the queen when he told her that he would do whatever she asked him to do. And again, the queen was against slavery, especially enslaving her own subjects. This is the same log entry where Columbus said, "Your Majesties will make Christians of them all, and that they will be **your** people, **which indeed I now hold them to be.**"

However, Columbus wasn't looking for trouble like a bully who loves to abuse innocent kids in school or a neighborhood. Columbus' approach to conquest was one of persuasion and alliance. Remember, he gave gifts to the natives for the sake of Christian charity, and to be perceived as a good person. He also promised Guacanagarí he would help him get rid of the cannibals after the chief helped him save the Santa María cargo. This is a form of covenant and alliance that everyone was familiar with, back then. It was normal for a weak tribe, or nation, to unite with a stronger one, so they could fight and defeat a common enemy. Here is an example, during Columbus' second voyage:

> [Columbus] then informed the [native] old man that **he had been sent thither by the King and Queen of Spain to take possession of those countries** hitherto unknown to the outside world, and that, moreover, **he would make war upon the cannibals and all the natives guilty of crimes,** punishing them according to their deserts. As for the innocent, he would protect and honour them because of their virtues. Therefore, neither he nor anyone whose intentions were pure need be afraid; rather, if he or any other honourable man had been injured in his interests by his neighbours he had only to say so. These words of the Admiral

afforded such pleasure to the old man that he announced that, although weakened by age, he would gladly go with Columbus, and he would have done so if his wife and sons had not prevented him. **What occasioned him great surprise was to learn that a man like Columbus recognized the authority of a sovereign**; but his astonishment still further increased when the interpreter explained to him how powerful were the kings and how wealthy, and all about the Spanish nation, the manner of fighting, and how great were the cities and how strong the fortresses. In great dejection the man, together with his wife and sons, threw themselves at the feet of Columbus, with their eyes full of tears, repeatedly asking if the country which produced such men and in such numbers was not indeed heaven (*De Orbe Novo* by Peter Martyr, The First Decade, Book III, p. 103).

Did you notice that the native "old man" understood what was going on? This wasn't foreign to him. He was also surprised with Columbus' loyalty to Spain.

On the calends of September he [Columbus] reached the port he had named San Nicholas, and there repaired his ships, intending to again ravage the cannibal islands and burn the canoes of the natives. He was determined that these rapacious wolves should no longer injure the sheep, their neighbours; but his project could not be realised because of his bad health (*De Orbe Novo* by Peter Martyr, The First Decade, Book III, p. 104).

Another cacique who was impressed with Columbus' power and how he went to destroy the cannibals' canoes, met him and told him that **before** he would "**take his land,**" he and his family would go with him and see Spain and its powerful monarchs. Columbus told him to stay instead as a vassal of the Sovereigns because he still had more places to explore (*Historia de los Reyes Católicos* by Andrés Bernáldez, Cap. CXXXXI, p. 329).

"Taking the land" did not mean the natives would be driven out from it, but that they would serve a new and more powerful king. My point here is that the natives knew what was happening. They were not strangers to the concept of conquest. The problem of Columbus seeking conquest by persuasion was that the Spaniards were not on the same page with him and ruined everything he planned.

Now, let's see some examples of conquest among the natives, during and after Columbus' time. In it, you will see natives joining other natives or Spaniards to fight a common enemy:

> But let us return to Caunaboa [Caonabó] who, if you remember, had been taken prisoner. This cacique, when he found himself put in irons, gnashed his teeth like an African lion and fell to thinking, night and day, upon the means to recover his liberty. He begged the Admiral, since the region of Cipangu was now under his authority, to send Spanish garrisons to protect the country **against the attacks of neighbors who were his ancient enemies** (*De Orbe Novo* by Peter Martyr, The First Decade, Book IV, p. 112).

Before Columbus initiated his third voyage, he left his brother in charge of Hispaniola, while he was in Spain:

> During this time the Adelantado [i.e. governor or mayor Bartholomew Columbus] who had marched to the right, had encountered at a place not far from the river Naiba **a powerful cacique, named Beuchios Anacauchoa, who was at that time engaged in an expedition to conquer the people along the river, as well as some other caciques of the island**. This powerful chieftain lives at the western extremity of the island, called Xaragua (*De Orbe Novo* by Peter Martyr, The First Decade, Book V, p. 118).

> [When Columbus returned, he] desiring to put a stop to the dangerous attacks of the Ciguana tribe which had revolted under the leadership of Guarionex, sent his brother the Adelantado with ninety foot-soldiers and some horsemen against them. **It may be truthfully added that about three thousand of the islanders who had suffered from the invasions of the Ciguana tribe, who were their sworn enemies, joined forces with the Spaniards** (*De Orbe Novo* by Peter Martyr, The First Decade, Book VII, p. 142).

These last three quotes will be expanded more in Chapter 31.

After Columbus' death, Peter Martyr tells us of a "time the wretched colonists of Darien liberated the cacique of Coiba, Careca, and even agreed to serve as his **allies** during a campaign against the cacique called Poncha, who was a neighbour of Careca on the continent" (*De Orbe Novo* by Peter Martyr, The Second Decade, Book III, p. 217).

In the previous chapter, we saw what the eldest son of Chief Comogre told the Spaniards about Indigenous slavery. Now let's see what the same native prince told the Spaniards about his Indigenous enemies and Indigenous conquest:

> King Tumanama will oppose your advance, for his is the richest kingdom of all. It lies six suns distant from ours (they count the days by suns); moreover you will encounter Carib tribes in the mountains, fierce people who live on human flesh, are subject to no law, and have no fixed country. They **conquered** the mountaineers for they coveted the gold mines, and for this reason they abandoned their own country (*De Orbe Novo* by Peter Martyr, The Second Decade, Book III, p. 221).

> The son of Comogre... spoke again as follows... 'Listen to me, Christians; we people who go naked are not tormented by covetousness, but we are **ambitious**, and we fight one against the other for power, each seeking to **conquer** his neighbour. This, therefore, is the source of **frequent wars** and of all our misfortunes. Our ancestors have been fighting men. Our father, Comogre, likewise fought with his neighbouring caciques, and we have been both **conquerors** and **conquered**. Just as you see prisoners of war amongst us, as for instance those seventy captives I have presented to you, so likewise have our enemies captured some of our people; for such are the fortunes of war' (*De Orbe Novo* by Peter Martyr, The Second Decade, Book III, p. 222).

Another tribe was described as "a **warlike race**, and have always been troublesome neighbours" (*De Orbe Novo* by Peter Martyr, The Third Decade, Book I, p. 285).

After Vasco Núñez de Balboa defeated a chief named Pacra, he won the friendship of the neighboring chiefs. One of them named Bononiama met Vasco to thank him.

> While speaking these words he raised his eyes to Heaven and gave it to be understood that he referred to the sun. 'In destroying our proud and **violent enemies** you have given peace to us and to all our people. You overcome monsters. We believe that you and your equally brave companions have been sent from Heaven, and under the protection of your machanes [or 'macana' which was the Indigenous word for 'sword' or 'club'] we may henceforth live without fear. Our gratitude to him who brings us these blessings and happiness shall be eternal.' Such, or something like this, was the speech of Bononiama, as translated by the interpreters. Vasco thanked him for having escorted our men and received them kindly, and sent him away loaded with precious gifts (*De Orbe Novo* by Peter Martyr, The Third Decade, Book II, p. 302).

During exploration in South America under Alonso de Hojeda, Juan de la Cosa and Amerigo Vespucci, Las Casas said that they described the natives as "a warrior tribe because they had very sharp weapons and were excellent marksmen... They... **call on one another** when they need to fight an enemy, who is usually an Indian of another language group who has killed one of them" (*History of the Indies* by Las Casas, Book One, Chapter 164, p. 63).

Any outrage about that? Where are the modern authors writing books condemning such behavior like they do with Columbus? Why do revisionists grumble when Columbus said, "with fifty men we could subjugate them all and make them do whatever we want," yet they don't say a word against the natives who were doing the same thing!? Dear reader, do you see the hypocrisy and the double standard of revisionists here as well?

Chapter 24. Amerigo vs. Columbus

Columbus went to Spain to defend himself against the complaints of Pedro Margarit and Friar Boyl, and now he is back in the New World on his third voyage where he discovers the South American continent. Some people assume that the American continent was named after Amerigo Vespucci because Amerigo discovered it. However, it was Columbus, and not Amerigo, who reached the continent first. Here is what Las Casas said about Amerigo on his expedition with Alonso de Hojeda:

> ... Columbus discovered the **continent**... Hojeda learned that Columbus had discovered the continent and saw the map... According to Americo Vespucci, Hojeda sailed from Santa Maria or Cadiz on May 20, 1497; **but this is a lie** -he sailed in 1499- told in order to claim the discovery of the continent for himself, thus usurping the glory and honor due to Columbus alone... Vespucci was in bad faith and deliberately sought to steal the admiral's glory... The admiral discovered the continent at Paria; Hojeda followed and Vespucci was with Hojeda who said they landed on Paria. The admiral had sailed from San Lucar on May 30, 1498; Hojeda and Vespucci must have sailed from Cadiz in 1499, because if Columbus left on May 30 and Hojeda on May 20, and Columbus sailed first, it is impossible

that Hojeda should leave in 1498. It cannot be argued that Hojeda sailed first, since Columbus was the first to arrive and discover Paria, which proves that Vespucci was mistaken when he said he sailed in 1497. He sailed in 1499, and it is clear that Columbus discovered the continent. It surprises me that the admiral's son, Hernando [i.e Ferdinand Columbus], who is such a wise man, did not notice how Americo Vespucci usurped the glory of his father, especially since he had documentary proof of it, as I know he does.

Las Casas added a footnote that says the continent "should have been called Columba [Columbia or Columbus] and not as it is unjustly called, America" (*History of the Indies* by Las Casas, Book One, Ch. 163, pp. 61-62).

In other words, Columbus arrived first and discovered **South** America. Amerigo Vespucci came later. As for who discovered North America and the mainland first, during this era, the evidence points at John Cabot.

In the words of Washington Irving:

... the person who first reached the mainland of the new world was most <u>probably</u> Sebastian [or his father John] Cabot, a native of Venice, sailing in the employ of England. In 1497 he coasted its shores from Labrador to Florida, yet neither the Venetians nor the English have set up any pretensions on his account to the disparagement of Columbus. His glory embraces the discovery of the whole western world; others may subdivide it and become illustrious upon portions: with respect to him, Vespucio is as Yáñez Pinzon, Bastides, Cabot, and the crowd of secondary discoverers that followed in his track. When Columbus first touched a shore of the new world, even though a frontier island, he had achieved his enterprize; he had accomplished all that was necessary for his fame; the great problem of the ocean was solved; the world that lay beyond its western waters was discovered. [1]

The same way the word **discover** doesn't mean "the first person to find desolate land" in Columbus' historical context, so it is with the name "America," or "New World." Neither one means just the United States. America includes North America, Central America, South America, and the Caribbean islands. "The New World is one of the names used for the Earth's Western Hemisphere, specifically the Americas (including nearby islands such as those of the Caribbean and Bermuda)." [2]

Las Casas himself said America was discovered in 1492, even though he knew Columbus didn't reach the continent that year. It is clear that for Las Casas the Caribbean was also America. He also said:

> The first that landed in this Kingdom when he discovered **America** was an Admiral [Columbus] well stricken in years, who had so hospitable and kind a reception from the aforesaid Guacanagari, as well as all those Spaniards that accompanied him in that Voyage... [3]

That's the historical context explaining why we say "Columbus discovered America." It is right and correct to say it, especially since because of him, and him alone, it was later learned that the continent was not Asia, "India," or the Indies, but rather, another continent.

An interesting observation is that Columbus, Vespucci, and Cabot were Italians, and all three of them worked for foreign countries: Columbus worked for Spain, Vespucci for Spain and Portugal, and John Cabot for England. Another observation, pertaining to how biased some modern "scholars" are, is that they all condemned Columbus for conquest and slavery, but they don't say a word about Vespucci or Cabot regarding those issues.

John Cabot:

And the before-named John [Cabot] and his sons, their heirs and assigns, may occupy and **possess** whatever towns, camps, cities, or islands may be discovered by them, that they may be able to **conquer**, occupy, and possess, as our vassals and governors, lieutenants or deputies, acquiring for us the dominion, title, and jurisdiction over these towns, camps, cities, islands, and mainlands so discovered (*Letters Patent granted to John Cabot and his Sons, March 5, 1496*). [4]

Having passed Ibernia, which is still further to the west, and then shaped a northerly course, he began to navigate to the eastern part, leaving (during several days) the North Star on the right hand; and having wandered thus for a long time, at length he hit upon land, where he hoisted the royal standard, and took **possession** for this Highness, and, having obtained various proofs of his discovery, he returned (*Second Despatch of Raimondo di Soncino to the Duke of Milan, December 18, 1497*). [5]

Amerigo Vespucci:

Vespucci and his men faced a warlike tribe in one of his explorations. They fought them and in Vespucci's own words:

> ... made about 250 of them captives, and we burnt the village, and returned to our ships with victory and 250 prisoners leaving many of them dead and wounded, and of ours there were no more than one killed, and 22 wounded, who all escaped (i-e., recovered), God be thanked... and we thereupon made sail for Spain with 222 captive **slaves**: and reached the port of Cadiz on the 15 day of October 1498, where we were well received and sold our **slaves**. Such is what befel me, most noteworthy, in this my first voyage (*Letter from Amerigo Vespucci to Pier Soderini of the Republic of Florence, First Voyage*). [6]

Where is the outcry against John Cabot for taking possession of foreign lands? Where is the outrage against Amerigo Vespucci for burning villages and selling natives as slaves? Why does Columbus get a "mixed legacy" label, but Cabot and Vespucci get a pass?

Chapter 25. The Spaniards vs. Columbus

Columbus' problem was the Spaniards and not the natives. When I say "the Spaniards" I don't mean Spain or their rulers, but those Spaniards who acted in jealousy, disobedience or mutiny toward him. This is a very important point to keep in mind, since Spain later became the target of political propaganda, stereotyping all Spaniards as "inherently evil."

Those Spaniards who hated him, hated him because he was not from Spain, and he was a stranger with no noble blood in him. Las Casas said they were arrogant, especially those who were highborn. "They **never** liked Columbus; therefore he had little credit with them" (*History of the Indies* by Las Casas, Book One, Ch. 92, p. 49).

From the very beginning Columbus struggled with these Spaniards. So let's review and expand this point in the story. Remember:

1. They mocked him at the Spanish council, before the discoveries.
2. The sailors threatened to throw him overboard on their way to the Caribbean.

During the first voyage:

3. Captain Martín Alonso Pinzón left the expedition to seek gold for himself without Columbus' permission (*Columbus' Journal,* translated by John Cummins, Wednesday, November 21, 1492).

4. On an island, Columbus had to send his secretary to prevent the Spaniards from committing fraud to the natives in their trade deals (*Columbus' Journal,* translated, by John Cummins, Saturday, December 22, 1492).

5. The disobedience of the crew of the Santa María caused the caravel to shipwreck on Christmas Eve (*Columbus' Journal,* translated by John Cummins, Tuesday, December 25, 1492).

6. Columbus left 39 men on Hispaniola with instructions to respect the natives, while he returned to Spain. The Spaniards disobeyed (*Columbus' Journal,* translated by John Cummins, Wednesday, January 2, 1492).

During the second voyage:

7. When Columbus returned to Hispaniola, he found his 39 men murdered by Caonabó for not respecting the natives and their wives as Columbus had instructed them to do (*The Life of the Admiral Christopher Columbus* by his son Ferdinand, Chapters 49-50).

8. Once the Spaniards' dreams of getting rich were quickly shattered, they attempted "to throw off the Admiral's authority, seize the remaining vessels, and return in them to Castile" *(The Life of the Admiral Christopher Columbus* by his son Ferdinand, Ch. 51, pp. 122-123).

9. The provisions Columbus brought from Spain were gone "partly because of poor management by the ship captains" (*The Life of the Admiral Christopher Columbus* by his son Ferdinand, Ch. 53, p. 128).

10.   While Columbus was busy exploring the Caribbean, the Spaniards were "busy" stealing and harassing natives in disobedience of Columbus' orders to keep peace with them. This led some natives to kill Spaniards in retaliation (*The Life of the Admiral Christopher Columbus* by his son Ferdinand, Ch. 61, pp. 147-148).

11.   Columbus decided to return to Spain because "envious men were giving the Sovereigns false accounts of what was happening in the Indies" (*The Life of the Admiral Christopher Columbus* by his son Ferdinand, Ch. 63, p. 169).

12.   On his way to Spain, the ship ran out of provisions and some Spaniards, "like Caribs, proposed to eat the Indians aboard," which Columbus forbade, saying, that "as Christians and human beings, they should not be treated worse than others." Of course, revisionists won't tell you that story either. (*The Life of the Admiral Christopher Columbus* by his son Ferdinand, Ch. 64, p. 173).

13.   In Seville, Columbus wanted to return immediately to Hispaniola, fearing for the welfare of the settlement, "especially since he had left them in great want of provisions... Ten or twelve months passed before he obtained the dispatch of two relief ships." The Spaniards delayed Columbus' third voyage departure "through neglect and mismanagement on the part of the royal officials." He also won Bishop Don Juan de Fonseca as a perpetual enemy at the Spanish court (*The Life of the Admiral Christopher Columbus* by his son Ferdinand, Ch. 65, pp. 173-174).

During the third voyage:

14.   Columbus discovered and reached the American continent. When he returned to Hispaniola he found the Spaniards in revolt against his brothers, whom he had left

there in charge. With "their provisions running short and suffering and sickness growing, they became discontented with their present lot and despair of the future. These disaffected persons making their complaints heard, there arose among them one who sought to stir up the others and make himself head of a faction." His name was Francisco Roldán (*The Life of the Admiral Christopher Columbus* by his son Ferdinand, Ch. 74, p. 191).

Roldan won over the crews by promising them fresh young girls instead of manual labour, pleasures instead of exertion, plenty in place of famine, and repose instead weariness and watching (*De Orbe Novo* by Peter Martyr, The First Decade, Book V, p. 128).

15. Columbus tried to fight the rebellion, but being outnumbered he ended up being humiliated and surrendered to the terms of the revolt ringleader, Roldán. The problem is that Roldán reaped what he had sown. He sowed rebellion, and he reaped rebellion back, as some of his own rebels revolted against him later (*The Life of the Admiral Christopher Columbus* by his son Ferdinand, Chapters 74-86).

16. "While these disorders went on, many of the rebels, writing from La Española, and others who had returned to Castile continually made false charges to the Catholic Sovereigns and their royal council against the Admiral and his brothers, claiming they were cruel and unfit to govern because they were foreigners and had no experiences in governing men of quality" (*The Life of the Admiral Christopher Columbus* by his son Ferdinand, Ch. 85, p. 220).

17. The Spanish Sovereigns sent Francisco de Bobadilla to investigate the allegations against Columbus, but Boba-

dilla arrested Columbus first and asked questions later. Bobadilla also confiscated Columbus' property and took the false testimonies from Columbus' enemies as "evidence," without any kind of verification (*The Life of the Admiral Christopher Columbus* by his son Ferdinand, Chapters 85-86).

Columbus wrote:

I never before heard of anyone who was commissioned to make an inquiry, assembling the rebels, and taking as evidence against their governor wretches without faith, and who are unworthy of belief (*Writings of Christopher Columbus*, p. 166).

Las Casas later added:

I have always believed they tried to depose the admiral in order to assume full government themselves because they were the kind of men who resent having a superior (*History of the Indies*, Book Three, Ch. 78, p. 206).

18. "As soon as the Catholic Sovereigns learned of the Admiral's arrival and that he came in chains, they gave orders... that he be placed at liberty... they decided to send out a governor to Española who should right the wrongs done to the Admiral and his brothers. Bobadilla should be commanded to make restitution of the Admiral's property... and the rebels were to be tried and punished as their offenses deserved" (*The Life of the Admiral Christopher Columbus* by his son Ferdinand, Ch. 87, p. 224).

During Columbus' fourth voyage:

19. Columbus and his men were marooned and stranded in Jamaica. He didn't let the Spaniards disperse onto the island, because he knew they were "by nature disrespectful" and "no punishment or order could have stopped them from running about the country and into the Indians' huts to steal what they found and commit outrages on their wives and children..." Guess what happened? Exactly! (*The Life of the Admiral Christopher Columbus* by his son Ferdinand, Ch. 101, pp. 265-266).

20. The mutineers went to steal from the natives and told them "to collect their pay from the Admiral and authorized them to kill him if he would not pay." Now Columbus had the Spaniards in rebellion and the natives as enemies again (*The Life of the Admiral Christopher Columbus* by his son Ferdinand, Ch. 102, p. 270).

21. Columbus' few crew allies defeated the mutineers. Columbus sent for help to Hispaniola, but the governor there sent a ship, not with the purpose of rescuing Columbus, but to spy on him. It is later that Columbus was rescued with his men, but the governor released "the ringleader of the mutiny, and proposed to punish those who had been responsible for his imprisonment" (*The Life of the Admiral Christopher Columbus* by his son Ferdinand, Chapters 103-108).

22. When Columbus returned from his fourth voyage, he found out the Queen of Spain had died. Columbus' property was still seized by the government, even though he was promised his property back. Now he had to beg for his rights, estate, and privileges to King Ferdinand, who was ignoring Columbus and trying to take them all away

(*The Life of the Admiral Christopher Columbus* by his son Ferdinand, Ch. 108).

On his deathbed Columbus died sick, depressed, forgotten, and unappreciated. Believe it or not, some revisionists deny this fact, but primary historical source Bartolomé de las Casas said it this way:

> So he died impecunious and in a state of great misery, not even owning a roof under which to rest his weary head, as he himself said, and this was the man who had discovered a New World, infinitely bigger and richer than the old. He died deposed of the status and fame he had won at the cost of incredible pains, dispossessed ignominiously and unjustly imprisoned without due process, judged by people seemingly acting as if they lacked reason, as if they were mad, stupid and absurd and worse than barbaric brutes (*History of the Indies,* Book Two, Ch. 38, p. 144).

Las Casas added that Columbus died still believing he was in Asian territory and not in another continent (*Historia de las Indias*, Tomo III, Lib. II, Cap. XXXVIII, p. 197).

Some conspiratorial revisionists assert Columbus knew he was in another continent. I guess they think they know more than Columbus and those who knew him well. I'm fascinated by how modern authors think they know more about what Columbus was thinking, than Columbus himself. To support their claims, they quoted Columbus saying, "I have come to believe that this is a mighty **continent which was hitherto unknown**" (*Historia de las Indias* by Las Casas, Tomo II, Lib. I, Cap. CXXXIX, p. 264).

But if you read two chapters after, you will see Columbus saying he believed the biblical Paradise was close or located in that land. How can that mean Columbus knew he was in **another** continent, when the biblical Paradise was in the Old World, and not the New one? "Unknown" meant the same as "New World;" that is, the place was "unknown" and "New" to him and the Spaniards during that period of time. It doesn't mean Columbus knew he was on another continent (*Historia de las Indias* by Las Casas, Tomo II, Lib. I, Cap. CXLI, p. 276).

Scholar Samuel Eliot Morison wrote that as Columbus was dying:

A priest was summoned, a Mass said, and everyone in this little circle of friends and relatives received the sacrament. The viaticum was administered to the dying Admiral; and after concluding prayer of his last office, remembering the last words of his Lord and Saviour, to whose sufferings he some-times ventured to compare his own, Columbus was heard to say *in manus tuas, Domine, commendo spiritum meum* [Lord, into your hands I commit my spirit]. 'And having said this, he gave up the ghost.' So died the man who had done more to direct the course of history... He had not found the Strait, or met the Grand Khan, or converted any great number of heathen, or regained Jerusalem. He had not even secured the future of his family. And the significance of what he had accomplished was only slightly less obscure to him than to the chroniclers who neglected to record his death, or to the courtiers who failed to attend his modest funeral at Valladolid. The vast extent and immense resources of the Americas were but dimly seen; the mighty ocean that laved their western shores had not yet yielded her secret. [1]

Wow! That's sad. Does anyone see the pattern of the Spaniards and Columbus' interaction here? Columbus was mocked, ridiculed, threatened, disrespected, disobeyed, hated, slandered, humiliated, underestimated, unjustly thrown into jail, and unappreciated at his death and burial. Columbus was trying to do something good, and he always tried to keep peace with the natives everywhere he went, but instead, the Spaniards destroyed everything he tried to build.

"I have now reached that point, that there is no man so vile but thinks it his right to insult me. The day will come when the world will reckon it as a virtue to him who has not given his consent to their abuse."
                -Christopher Columbus

Chapter 26. Mutilations, Cruelty and Fake Biography

Many Columbus' biographies, including encyclopedias and the like, are very accurate with Columbus' story, until they reach the part where he and his brothers were falsely accused of atrocities. The reason is that many of them are repeating the accusations made by Columbus' enemies as "historical facts" without telling the reader the accusations were false. Some of these false testimonies came from the slanderous accusations made during Roldán's rebellion, and later by others during a lawsuit known as the *Pleitos*, even though primary historical sources like Bartolomé de las Casas, clearly stated, they were "convincingly false" (*History of the Indies* by Las Casas, Book One, Ch. 34, p. 34. *Historia de las Indias* by Las Casas, Tomo I, Lib. I, Cap. XXXIV, p. 257).

Can you imagine theologians writing Jesus' biography from the point of view of his contemporary enemies, the Pharisees? It would be something like "Jesus didn't rise from the dead," "his body was stolen by his disciples," or that Jesus was a "false prophet!" Ridiculous! That is exactly the way Columbus' biography is being retold today. This is where we hear the lies like, "there was no gold in Hispaniola," which we already debunked, or that Columbus and his brothers abused natives and Spaniards alike. Just look at how the History Channel characterized Columbus' third voyage:

He visited Trinidad and the South American mainland before returning to the ill-fated Hispaniola settlement, where the colonists had staged a bloody revolt against the **Columbus brothers' mismanagement and brutality**. Conditions were so bad that Spanish authorities had to send a new governor to take over. Christopher Columbus was arrested and returned to Spain in chains. [1]

In 2006, The Guardian reported that a 48-page long document was found where "Christopher Columbus, the man credited with discovering the Americas, was a greedy and **vindictive tyrant** who saved some of his most violent punishments for his own followers... Punishments included cutting off people's ears and noses, parading women naked through the streets and selling them into slavery." [2]

Guess who wrote that "lost" document? The answer is Francisco de Bobadilla, who we just mentioned in the previous chapter and whose testimonies were proven false. Bobadilla replaced Columbus as governor, and the Spaniards loved him because he let Spaniards do whatever they wanted with the natives. Las Casas said the Spaniards "adored him... because they knew how much freer they were" without Columbus (*History of the Indies* by Las Casas, Book Two, Ch. 1, p. 79).

That's the Bobadilla character we are supposed to believe. Now, let's talk about mutilations and torture for a moment: Punishment for crimes by inflicting pain or injury, including flogging, branding and even mutilation, was practiced in most civilizations since ancient times. [3] Don't forget the crucifixions by the Romans, the harshness of Sharia law, or the Torah, when it said, "If two men are fighting and the wife of one of them comes to rescue her husband from his assailant, and she reaches out and seizes him by his private parts, you shall cut off her hand. Show her no pity." Deuteronomy 25:11-12 (NIV).

Marco Polo, whose travels inspired Columbus, described the way the Tartars administered justice. He said:

> When any one has committed a petty theft, they give him, under the orders of authority, seven blows of a stick, or seventeen, or twenty-seven, or thirty-seven, or forty- seven, and so forth, always increasing by tens in proportion to the injury done, and running up to one hundred and seven. Of these beatings sometimes they die. But if the offence be horse-stealing, or some other great matter, they cut the thief in two with a sword. [4]

Marco Polo lived almost two hundred years before Columbus, so let me give you one more example of punishment, but this time, from Columbus' times. In 1492, King Ferdinand was stabbed with a knife, but he survived. How did they punish the person who attempted to kill him? First, they cut the hand he used for the stabbing; then with hot iron pincers, they removed one nipple and one eye. Next, they cut his other hand, removed his other nipple and the other eye. They cut off his nose, his feet, his members, and his heart. They then threw the body outside of the city, where they stoned him, burned his body, and finally threw his ashes to the wind (*Historia de los Reyes Católicos* by Andrés Bernáldez, Cap. CXVI, p. 267).

It is true this man was punished severely because the person he tried to kill was no other than the king. But it is also true that cutting ears or noses off was a way some crimes were punished during this period of time. Las Casas said he "even knew one whose ears had been cut off for a crime in Castile" (*History of the Indies* by Las Casas, Book One, Ch. 112, p. 60).

Some Indigenous tribes did likewise or worse.

If you think this is barbaric, it's because it was. Columbus' time was during the end of the Medieval period, merging with the Renaissance. These were not politically correct times in Europe or anywhere else in the world. Like conquest and slavery, Columbus was imparting justice the way people had been administering justice for thousands of years before him.

The question is: Did Columbus (and his brothers) use the punishments of his day to punish lawbreakers or to torture innocent victims? That's the question. The answer is: Columbus was a man of integrity, and he and his brothers punished lawbreakers the way justice was imparted in his day.

How did Columbus punish people?

Las Casas said in Chapter 92 of his *Historia* that Columbus "had to use violence" against the Spaniards, but he didn't specify how (*History of the Indies*, Book One, p. 49).

Ferdinand Columbus told us that he (Columbus) punished them with jail and low rations of food (*The Life of the Admiral Christopher Columbus* by his son Ferdinand, Ch. 47, p. 114).

None of the primary historical sources say anything about Columbus personally cutting ears or noses off. Michele de Cuneo (whose account has a number of inaccuracies) says that some Spaniards were punished in that manner for some illegal activity they were engaged in secret. **Columbus is not mentioned there by name**, but since he was the leader, it could be assumed he **might** be the one behind the punishment. See *Journals and Other Documents on the Life and Voyages of Christopher Columbus* by Morison, p. 215.

We also know he hung some of Roldán's former confederates, during the rebellion of his third voyage (*Historia General* by Herrera, Década I, Lib. IV, Cap. VIII, p. 110).

16th-century historian, López de Gómara, confirms the same. That is, that Columbus hanged and whipped many Spaniards for abusing the natives (*Historia General de las Indias* by Gómara, Cap. XX, p. 56).

Don't forget that it was the queen herself who commanded Columbus to severely punish the Spaniards for misbehaving toward the natives. However, there is no evidence of a woman's tongue being cut off for suggesting Columbus was of low birth as the Guardian article claims on their website. There is no evidence of Columbus punishing anyone without criminal cause either.

I want to remind you that these Spaniards who Columbus punished, were the same ones who mistreated the natives. They stole from them, raped them, beat them, whipped them, cut their ears off and killed them for no reason whatsoever. See *Historia de las Indias* by Las Casas, Tomo II, Lib. I, Chapters CLV, CLIX and CLXI.

I don't know why anyone should feel sorry for them, especially since their abuses was the cause of the depopulation of a great number of natives after Columbus was removed from office! See Chapter 28.

Bartolomé de las Casas also made a similar observation when he said, that the "punishments and damages that many claimed" Columbus "committed against them, they perhaps deserved, because of their crimes, insults, disobedience, and sins" ("... quizás los castigos y daños hechos, que á muchos dicen que hizo, los merecían por sus delitos, insultos ó inobediencias y pecados..." *Historia de las Indias* by Las Casas, Tomo II, Lib. I, Cap. CLXXXIII, pp. 513-514).

Another lie by Columbus' enemies and repeated today as *fact* by some is that Columbus kept the natives from baptism so he could keep more of them as slaves. Remember, Spanish law wouldn't allow one to sell Christians as slaves. Of course, the charge is ridiculous, and even Las Casas, who was critical of Columbus at times, defended Columbus on this point. Las Casas said that it would have been a sacrilege "to give baptism to anyone who doesn't know what he received." ("Que no consentía que se baptizasen los indios que querían los clérigos y frailes baptizar, porque quería más esclavos que cristianos; pero esto podia impedir justamente, si los querían baptizar sin doctrina, porque era gran sacrilegio dar el baptismo á quien no sabia lo que rescibia." *Historia de las Indias* by Las Casas, Tomo II, Lib. I, Cap. CLXXX, p. 493).

Washington Irving commented that this "last charge, so contrary to the pious feelings of the admiral, was founded on his having objected to the baptism of certain Indians of mature age, until they could be instructed in the doctrines of Christianity; justly considering it an abuse of that holy sacrament to administer it thus blindly." [5]

Others had claimed **Columbus** used dogs to hunt natives instead of foxes as a "pastime." This claim is another example of revisionists distorting the facts by attributing atrocities committed by the Spaniards on Columbus. The Spaniards abused the natives in that fashion, but years later, after Columbus was already out of office, or dead. [6]

Columbus did use dogs, but **only** for WAR, in self-defense, or to find rebel natives who would hide in the mountains. The police today still use dogs to find runaway prisoners or to fight criminals. This is not foreign, or strange. See *The Life of the Admiral Christopher Columbus* by his son Ferdinand, Ch. 61, p. 149.

Columbus had an iron hand when it came to crime, yet, neither him, nor his brothers, were vindictive, or cruel "Nazis" like some people want us to believe today. Here are some examples:

1.   When Columbus touched land for the very first time on his first voyage, the sailors who threatened his life were now kissing his hands begging for forgiveness. He forgave them and it seems he even left that part out of the story in his journal, since those who have attempted to reconstruct the

lost journal, usually left that part out. We know that part of the story today because the other primary historical sources wrote about it. That doesn't sound like a vindictive person. See *Historia de las Indias* by Las Casas, Tomo I, Lib. I, Cap. XL, p. 292. Also *Historia General y Natural* by Oviedo, Lib. II, Cap. V, p. 24.

2. After Pinzón returned from pursuing gold on his own without Columbus' permission, Columbus decided to forgive him because, in his own words, he did not wish "to assist Satan in his evil work and his desire to hinder" the voyage (*Columbus' Journal*, translated by John Cummins, Sunday, January 6, 1493).

3. As mentioned in Chapter 17, Columbus forgave several natives who were sentenced to death, at the pleadings of another cacique (*The Life of the Admiral Christopher Columbus* by his son Ferdinand, Ch. 53, p. 129).

4. Columbus reduced the tribute he made the natives to pay because he felt mercy for them. Do you think Hitler or Himmler would have done that? Or would they have raised the price of the tribute instead? See *Historia General* by Herrera, Década I, Lib. II, Cap. XVII, p. 61. Also *Historia de las Indias* by Las Casas, Tomo II, Lib. I, Cap. CV, p.104.

5. Columbus' brother went to meet one of the caciques of Hispaniola and was received with music, dancing, and a blood sport that was so violent, that he asked them to stop. If Columbus' brother was so bloodthirsty, as revisionists claim, why was he not enjoying the violent show natives put on for him? See *Historia de las Indias* by Las Casas, Tomo II, Lib. I, Cap. CXIV, pp. 139-140.

6. After arresting Chief Guarionex for conspiracy, Bartholomew Columbus (Columbus' brother), let him go free after Guarionex's people came unarmed, crying and begging for the life and release of their leader. Las Casas

said, Bartholomew Columbus "felt compassion for them," and let Guarionex go. Do you think Hitler would have felt compassion for anyone begging for mercy? See *Historia de las Indias* by Las Casas, Tomo II, Lib. I, Cap. CXV, p. 145.

7. If Columbus was so unrepentant, why did he constantly take communion? See Chapter 4.

8. If Columbus was so resentful, why did he warn his enemies at Hispaniola that a hurricane was coming their way during his fourth voyage? These were the same enemies who earlier revolted against him and unjustly put him in prison (*The Life of the Admiral Christopher Columbus* by his son Ferdinand, Ch. 88, p. 228).

9. If Columbus was so vindictive, why did he grant a full pardon (with the exception of the ringleader) to the mutineers, who wanted to kill him, during his fourth voyage? *The Life of the Admiral Christopher Columbus* by his son Ferdinand, Ch. 107, p. 281.

This is what Columbus wrote about that particular episode:

> There were deaths and many wounded but finally the Lord, who abhors arrogance and ungratefulness, delivered all them into our hands. I forgave them and agreed to reinstate them in all their honors... (*History of the Indies* by Las Casas, Book Two, Ch. 36, p. 136).

There was only one incident... let me repeat that again, there was only ONE incident where Columbus lost his composure and attacked a man named Ximeno, who was harassing him,

while Columbus was getting ready for his third voyage (*Historia de las Indias* by Las Casas, Tomo II, Lib. I, Cap. CXXVI, p. 199.
Washington Irving said the following about the incident:

> Nothing could demonstrate more strongly what Columbus had previously suffered from the machinations of unworthy men, than this transport of passion, **so unusual in his well-governed temper. He deeply regretted it**, and in a letter written some time afterwards to the sovereigns, he entreated that it might not be allowed to injure him in their opinion, he being "absent, envied, and a stranger. [7]

If Columbus was a "Nazi," or so vindictive, why would he regret anything? Or, is it that the charges against him, by past and present enemies, are all false? Columbus was described by both, Ferdinand Columbus and Bartolomé de las Casas, as "patient, long-suffering" and "prone to forgive injuries" as stated in Chapter 4.

Another false accusation by his enemies of the past, and repeated by his present enemies is, that he was not a good governor.

> ... many of the rebels... made **false charges** to the Catholic Sovereigns and their royal council against the Admiral and his brothers, claiming they were cruel and unfit to govern because they were foreigners and had no experience in governing **men of quality** (*The Life of the Admiral Christopher Columbus* by his son Ferdinand, Ch. 85, p. 220).

"Men of quality"? Really? Even some pro-Columbus people believe that he was an awesome explorer, but a terrible governor. On the surface, it looked like that, especially since he couldn't control the Spaniards. Nevertheless, if anyone takes the time to study Columbus' life, one could see that he had the traits of a good leader. For example, he was a man of integrity and not a corrupt politician. He was loyal to God and he always looked to honor and please the Spanish Sovereigns, even though he was a foreigner. A good leader delegates, and he always did, whenever he went to explore the New World. The Spaniards didn't like that he later delegated the leadership of the island to his brothers, but Columbus' brothers were the only ones who were not harassing the natives when he was not around.

Columbus always would think of every detail for his travels. Everything he asked for from the King and Queen of Spain, he was granted, and praised for his wise decisions. The king and queen responded to him with, "he has done well," "this is well and exactly as he should do," "the Admiral has done well," etc. Not bad for someone without "political experience." See *Select Letters of Christopher Columbus*, pp. 72-107.

The Hispaniola settlement sometimes lacked provisions and food due to the tardiness of the Spanish bureaucracy, and not because of Columbus. The struggles with the natives were always caused by the Spaniards, not Columbus. A good leader asks for help when he needs help. When Columbus couldn't control the Spaniards' behavior, he "sent envoys to inform the sovereigns of the revolt, begging them at the same time to send soldiers to put down the insurrection and punish the guilty, according to their crimes" (*De Orbe Novo* by Peter Martyr, The First Decade, Book VII, p. 141).

He also asked the kings to send "two virtuous people for council," and other people who could help him with the leadership of the island (*Historia de las Indias* by Las Casas, Tomo II, Libro I, Cap. CLX, p. 370).

Las Casas disagreed with Ferdinand Columbus on this, because he believed Columbus and his brothers "did not show modesty and discretion in governing the Spaniards." I don't know what Las Casas wanted Columbus and his brothers to do! If they had not punished the Spaniards, they would have been criticized for letting them harass the natives. But if they had punished them like they did, they would be criticized anyway for being *too harsh*. It's easy to criticize someone, when you are not in their shoes. The reason why Columbus seemed to *fail* as governor is because he never got the help he requested on time; thus, the rebels took control and did whatever they wanted to do with him and the natives (*Historia de las Indias* by Las Casas, Tomo II, Lib. I, Cap. CLXXX, p. 495).

In summary, Columbus' actual biography contradicts the false accusations from his past and present enemies. The false biographies say Columbus enslaved the natives because "there was no gold," when there was gold, and he did not enslave anyone for that reason. It says, he was a "Nazi," when he was not. It says, he was *vindictive*, when he wasn't. It says, he "tortured innocent victims," when he did not. It says, "he kept the natives from baptism," when it wasn't true. It says he was a *bad leader*, when he was the adult in the room.

Chapter 27. The Imaginary Child Sex Slavery Ring

The most outrageous of the accusations against Columbus, and maybe the most fictional, is that Columbus ran some kind of child sex slavery ring or sold children for sex. This garbage was for some time on a handful of websites. Thankfully, some of them have removed it. The so-called "evidence" for this charge is a quote (out of its context) from a letter, that in the words of The Huffington Post, Columbus "casually wrote about it in his log." [1] Here is the quote:

> For one woman they give a hundred castellanos, as for a farm; and this sort of trading is very common, and there are already a great number of merchants who go in search of girls; there are at this moment some nine or ten on sale; they fetch a good price, let their age be what it will (Letter to Juana de las Torres by Columbus, from *Writings of Christopher Columbus*, p. 165).

In the first place, Columbus was not "casually" writing about it, as The Huffington Post claimed. Instead, he was on his way to jail in Spain after Bobadilla unjustly arrested him without due process. Second, there is <u>NOTHING</u> about pedophilia in that letter. Some people assume sex was implied because revisionists only show you the line that says merchants were looking for girls, and they misread the numbers "nine or ten" as the ages of the young women. But the quote says, <u>merchants</u> (and not Columbus) were looking for young women (not young children) they could sell as slaves. It doesn't say they were looking for women they could have sex with. As a matter of fact, the Spaniards would have sex with native women whether they were free or slaves, with their consent or by force. They didn't need a clandestine ring for that. However, there is not one drop of evidence of pedophilia.

The letter was written in 1500 and was addressed to a female friend of Columbus named Juana de las Torres, who was also a friend of the queen. Can you imagine the reaction of Columbus' friend, as a woman, to learn he was selling little girls for sex? And why would Columbus write such an incriminating statement to a woman who was also a friend of the queen?

Fray Las Casas himself did not condemn the quote as evidence of pedophilia or a sex slave trade, which he would have done since he was the defender of the natives' human rights.

So, what is the content and context of the letter? In the letter Columbus complained against the Spaniards' corruption, how he had been harassed by people like Yañez Pinzón, Juan Aguado, and Alonso de Hojeda. He also mentions another rebellion led by a man named Adrián Mojica; he talks about how Bobadilla took the governorship of the island, how he confiscated his property and arrested him without due process. This is where Columbus sarcastically said, "Now that so much gold is found, these people stop to consider whether they can obtain the greatest quantity of it by **theft**, or by going to the mines." Incidentally, that's the line before the imaginary "child sex ring."

In other words, those were the actions of the SPANIARDS, and not Columbus. Columbus was denouncing them, not applauding them. The Spaniards sought women they could sell as slaves under Roldán's and/or Bobadilla's leadership. They had usurped Columbus' power during the rebellions. Spaniards were doing whatever they wanted with the natives and gold. See *The Life of the Admiral Christopher Columbus* by his son Ferdinand, Chapters 77-85.

Remember, Columbus had been authorized to temporarily enslave only those he would defeat in war. This is very different from merchants seeking people, in this case women, for the sole purpose of selling them as slaves.

In another letter Columbus described these groups of people as, "debauchees, profligates, thieves, seducers, ravishers, vagabonds." He also said:

They respected nothing and were perjurers and liars, already condemned by the tribunals, or fearful, owing to their numerous crimes, to appear before them. They had formed a faction amongst themselves, given over to violence and rapine; lazy, gluttonous, caring only to sleep and to carouse. They spared nobody; and having been brought to the island of Hispaniola originally to do the work of miners or of camp servants, they now never moved a step from their houses on foot, but insisted on being carried about the island upon the shoulders of the unfortunate natives, as though they were dignitaries of the State. Not to lose practice in the shedding of blood, and to exercise the strength of their arms, they invented a game in which they drew their swords, and amused themselves in cutting off the heads of innocent victims with one sole blow. Whoever succeeded in more quickly landing the head of an unfortunate islander on the ground with one stroke, was proclaimed the bravest, and as such was honoured (*De Orbe Novo* by Peter Martyr, The First Decade, Book VII, p. 142).

That's the kind of people Columbus was speaking against while appealing to the queen for justice. Some revisionists also claim that when Columbus was arrested, he admitted some of his "crimes" when he faced the Spanish monarchs in chains. I wonder where they got that information from, because even in the Juana de las Torres letter, Columbus said he wasn't told what he was charged for, and all he did in that letter was to reproach the Spaniards instead. Columbus knew Bobadilla persuaded the Spaniards to write falsehoods about him "such as were never invented in hell" (that's Columbus' own words), but he did not know why he was arrested (*Select Letters of Christopher Columbus*, p. 163).

Columbus wrote:

I have never spoken with him [Bobadilla], and to this day he has not permitted anyone to hold converse with me, and I make oath that I have no conception for what cause I am made prisoner (*Letter to Juana de las Torres* from *Writings of Christopher Columbus*, p. 168).

The only "apology" non-apology he gave in the letter was when he wrote:

I know, assuredly, that the **errors** which I **may** have fallen into have been done without the intention to do wrong, and I think that their Highnesses will believe me when I say so... **IF** I have been in **error**, it has been innocently and under the force of circumstances, as they will shortly understand beyond all doubt (Letter to Juana de las Torres by Columbus, from *Writings of Christopher Columbus*, p. 174).

Columbus didn't mention or admit any crimes or atrocities in the letter because he didn't commit any. Since he was on his way to jail, he assumed there was a reason for it, thus the possibility of error on his part.

When Columbus met the King and Queen of Spain, he didn't admit to any crimes or atrocities either because he didn't commit any. What happened instead was he was so humiliated that he could not utter a word for a while. Then he exploded and burst into sobbing and tears at the feet of the king and queen. That was his "confession"! When he was able to speak, he told the sovereigns how much he always sought to serve them faithfully, and he never meant to bring any offense to them. The king and queen replied to Columbus with kindness and grace assuring him his "imprisonment had not been by their wishes or command." Eventually, the Spanish monarchs removed Bobadilla out of office, and imprisoned Roldán and his accomplices.

That's how the story ended: Without imaginary child sex slavery rings, without confession of crimes, and with the real criminals in jail. Columbus was promised his titles and property back and soon thereafter he would make his fourth and last voyage to the New World. See *The Life of the Admiral Christopher Columbus* by his son Ferdinand, Ch. 87. *Historia General* by Herrera, Década I, Lib. IV, Cap. X, p. 116. Also *Historia de las Indias* by Las Casas, Tomo II, Lib. 1, Cap. CLXXXIII, p. 512.

Chapter 28. Genocide

It sounds incredible, but many natives died by something close to a *genocide*. This is the charge that is used to compare Columbus to Hitler, or Himmler.

Ward Churchill said, "Columbus was never a head of state. Comparisons of him to Nazi SS leader Heinrich Himmler, rather than Hitler, are therefore more accurate and appropriate." Except, the "head of the state" (the Queen of Spain) was against the mistreatment of natives, and Columbus was in charge of punishing those who harassed them. Churchill is wrong in his comparison. Besides, the beginning of Hispaniola's *genocide* was caused by the Spaniards under the leadership of Nicolás de Ovando while Columbus was exploring the continent in Central and South America during his fourth and last voyage.

The word *genocide* also gives the impression that ALL the natives everywhere were murdered, which it's not true either. If that was the case, why do we still have Indigenous tribes in North, Central, and South America? Why do we have so many dark-skinned people in Central and South America? Apart from the existing tribes, Hispanics are descendants of the Indigenous tribes that existed during Columbus' time.

The question is, who were the victims of *genocide*? The answer is, most natives in the Caribbean, starting with Hispaniola under Governor Ovando. That's why we see today that half of Hispaniola island (Haití) is populated by black people of African descent, while the other half of the island (The Dominican Republic) is populated with more of a mixed-race. If you visit the island next to Hispaniola, Puerto Rico, you will see that we are a melting pot of natives, blacks, and European peoples, with hardly any surviving native culture or native language. The same is with Cuba. In Jamaica, most people are black, and the same is with many islands in the Bahamas. All this is due to the Spaniards raiding the islands and abusing the natives until most of them were exterminated, leaving just a handful of them alive.

Returning where we left off the story, Columbus was pardoned by the Spanish kings, because he was innocent of all charges. The king and queen replaced Bobadilla with Nicolás de Ovando as the new governor, who arrested Roldán and his rebels and shipped them back to Spain, but the ship sank and most of Columbus' enemies died. It was as if an act of Divine judgment took place, but it was interpreted as a *spell* cast by Columbus in the eyes of contemporary superstitious men. See *History of the Indies* by Las Casas, Book Two, Ch. 3, p. 83, and *The Life of the Admiral Christopher Columbus* by his son Ferdinand, Ch. 88, p. 228.

Queen Isabel declared all the natives free from slavery under the new governor, Nicolás de Ovando; except Ovando didn't let them know they were free. If Columbus would have been the governor in this period of time, the natives would have been set free for sure. Instead, Ovando complained to the king saying that the natives were *lazy* and the lack of communication with them as free men kept them from Christian teaching. Of course, that is nonsense. Sadly, the sovereigns bought into it and replied with the following statement: Entice "the cacique and his men to work as freemen and not as slaves... they must be given wages [i.e. get paid], they must be treated well... allowing no one to harm or displeased them in any way, etc." (*History of the Indies* by Las Casas, Book Two, Ch. 11, pp. 103-104 and Ch. 12, p. 106).

Ovando was deceptive and did whatever he wanted with the natives. When it came to religion, Las Casas said, "that in the nine years the comendador [or Commander Ovando] governed the island, no measures were taken for the conversion of Indians" (*History of the Indies* by Las Casas, Book Two, Ch. 13, p. 109).

When it came to "work as freemen," Ovando exterminated most of them in a few years, under the "Encomiendas" system. This is where we get the famous revisionist lines they attribute to Columbus, like:

> Thus husbands and wives were together only once every eight or ten months and when they met they were so exhausted and depressed on both sides... they ceased to procreate. As for the newly born, they died early because their mothers, overworked and famished, had no milk to nurse them, and for this reason, while I was in **Cuba**, 7000 children died in three months.

Note, that though Columbus explored Cuba, he never settled there, so this is more evidence that the quote above is not about Columbus. Las Casas continued:

> Some mothers even drowned their babies from sheer desperation... In this way, husbands died in the mines, wives died at work, and children died from lack of milk... and in a short time this land which was so great, so powerful and fertile... was depopulated... (*History of the Indies* by Las Casas, Book Two, Ch. 13, p. 110).

And:

My eyes have seen these acts so foreign to human nature, and now I tremble as I write... (*History of the Indies* by Las Casas, Book Two, Ch. 17, p. 121).

Or the cutting the hands of natives, "leaving the skin dangling," mentioned in Chapter 19. See *History of the Indies* by Las Casas, Book Two, Ch. 15, p. 118.

It was in this period, and not during Columbus' leadership as revisionists claim, that natives committed mass suicides by poisoning themselves "drinking the juice of cassava root" and pregnant women would abort their children with certain herbs (*History of the Indies* by Las Casas, Book Two, Ch. 40, p. 146, and *Historia de las Indias* by Las Casas, Tomo III, Lib. II, Cap. XL, p. 206).

Peter Martyr confirmed the above by saying:

... there is one point which causes me small satisfaction; these simple, naked natives were little accustomed to labour, and the immense fatigues they now suffer, labouring in the mines, is killing them in great numbers and reducing the others to such a state of despair that many kill themselves, or refuse to procreate their kind. It is alleged that the pregnant women take drugs to produce abortion, knowing that the children they bear will become the slaves of the Christians. Although a royal decree has declared all the islanders to be free, they are forced to work more than is fit for free men. The number of these unfortunate people diminishes in an extraordinary fashion. Many people claim that they formerly numbered more than twelve millions; how many there are today I will not venture to say, so much am I horrified (*De Orbe Novo*, The Third Decade, Book VIII, p. 376).

All these are cruelties revisionists attribute to Columbus in popular memes on the Internet, when in reality they were committed by Ovando and his corrupted Spaniards. All these actions were against the queen's knowledge, consent, and legislation. Don't forget Columbus, himself, punished the Spaniards and complained against them for abusing the natives.

In his biography of Bartolomé de las Casas, Francis Augustus MacNutt wrote:

> The Spanish sovereigns were honestly desirous of protecting their new subjects, and the injustice inflicted on the latter was done in defiance of the laws they enacted, as well as of public opinion in Spain, which condemned it as severely as could the most advanced humanitarian sentiment of our own times. [1]

Believe it or not, some modern authors have said, Bobadilla and Ovando were better governors than Columbus!

Washington Irving made a contrast between Governor Columbus and Governor Ovando. He wrote:

> Such was the ruthless system which had been pursued during the absence of the admiral, by the commander Ovando, this man of boasted prudence and moderation, who was sent to reform the abuses of the island, and, above all, to redress the wrongs of the natives. The system of Columbus may have borne hard upon the Indians, born and brought up in untasked freedom, but it was never cruel nor sanguinary. He inflicted no wanton massacres, nor vindictive punishments; his desire was to cherish and civilize the Indians, and render them useful

subjects; not to oppress, and persecute and destroy them. When he came to behold the desolation that had thus swept them from the land during his suspension from authority, he could not retain the strong expression of his feelings. In a letter written to the king after his return to Spain, he thus expresses himself on the subject. 'The Indians of Hispaniola were, and are the riches of the island; for it is they who cultivate and make the bread and other provisions for the Christians; who dig the gold from the mines, and perform all the offices and labours both of man and of beasts of burthen. I am informed that since I left this island six parts out of seven of the natives are dead; all through **ill-treatment and inhumanity;** some by the sword, others by blows and cruel usage, others through hunger. The greater part have perished in the mountains and glens, whither they had fled, from not being able to support the labour imposed upon them.' For his own part, he added, although he had sent many Indians to Spain to be sold, it was always with a view to their being instructed in the Christian faith, and in civilized arts and usages, and afterwards sent back to their native island to assist in civilizing their countrymen. The brief view that has been given of the policy of Ovando on certain points on which Columbus was censured, may enable the reader to judge more correctly of the conduct of the latter. It is not to be measured by the standard of right and wrong established in the present more enlightened age. We must consider him in connexion with the era in which he lived. By comparing his measures with those of men of his own times, praised for their virtues and abilities, placed in precisely his own situation, and placed there expressly to correct his faults, we shall be the better enabled to judge how virtuously and wisely, under the peculiar circumstances of the case, he may be considered to have governed. [2]

"I have greatly sinned. Yet, every time that I have asked, I have been covered by the mercy and compassion of Our Lord. I have found the sweetest consolation in throwing off all my cares in order to contemplate his marvellous presence."
                    -Christopher Columbus

Chapter 29. Constructive Criticism

Columbus was a hero indeed, but he had his share of imperfections and shortcomings like anyone else. Constructive criticism is good, but slander is not. Revisionists didn't have to lie about Columbus to find out that he had a handful of bad choices on his hands. Even a primary historical source, Bartolomé de las Casas, had a few things to say against Columbus. Revisionists could have easily quoted Las Casas' disapproval of some of Columbus' actions if they wanted to criticize him, but they chose to misquote Las Casas' book, *History of the Indies,* attributing Governor Ovando and the Spaniards' atrocities to Columbus. Perhaps the reason why revisionists won't talk about Columbus' real negative actions is because none of them have anything to do with racism and genocide, or because some of them are not that serious if one takes the historical setting into consideration. So let's take a look at some examples of constructive criticism for Columbus:

1. Out of Wedlock- Starting with Columbus' personal life, Columbus was a widower and a single father of one son when he reached Spain from Portugal in 1485. However, while he was in Spain (before he launched his voyages) he had a son out of wedlock with a woman named Beatriz Enríquez de Arana. Nevertheless, Columbus raised his son as his own, and that son, Ferdinand Columbus, became his biographer, who also accompanied him on his fourth

voyage. Scholar John Cummins believed that "Columbus never married Beatriz, probably because he thought it socially disadvantageous. The stresses of life and voyaging separated them, but she remained in Columbus's mind to the last; he took care to support her financially, and in his will he mentioned his great debt to her and his heavy conscience. He made no specific bequest to her, but asked Diego [Columbus' eldest son] to look to her welfare." [1]

2. Kidnapping- One thing Columbus did in all of his voyages was to take natives by force.

> On my arrival at that sea I had taken some Indians by force from the first island that I came to, in order that they might learn our language, and com-municate to us what they knew respecting the country; which plan succeeded excellently, and was a great advantage to us, for in a short time, either by gestures and signs, or by words, we were enabled to understand each other (*Writings of Christopher Columbus*, p. 42).

The captured natives were also his evidence to Spain that he went to the Indies and not to some other place. Some of the captured natives escaped from Columbus during the first voyage, so he decided to change tactics. This time, he would capture them, give them gifts, and let them go, so they could see Columbus had good intentions. Remember, Columbus didn't know their language, and the natives didn't know his. Columbus wrote:

> By now another small almadia was approaching the Niña from a different headland with one man in it who had come to barter a ball of cotton. He did not

want to come aboard, so some of the sailors jumped into the sea and captured him. I saw all this from the deck of the sterncastle, so I sent for him; I gave him a red bonnet and put a few little green glass beads on his arm and hung two bells from his ears. I had him put back in his almadia, which had also been taken aboard the ship's boat, and sent him back ashore... When the man to whom I had given gifts, refusing his ball of cotton, reached the shore I saw that all the others came up to him. He was amazed and thought that we were good people and that the other who had escaped was being taken with us because he had done us some harm. That was my purpose in giving him presents and letting him go: to make them think well of us, so that when Your Majesties send someone else here he may be well received (*Columbus' Journal*, translated by John Cummins, Monday, October 15, 1492).

On the way they came across an old man who had not been able to run away. They captured him but told him that they wished him no harm and gave him a few oddments of barter goods, then they let him go. I wish I had seen him, so as to have given him some clothes and asked him questions... (*Columbus' Journal*, translated by John Cummins, Thursday, November 29, 1492).

We came suddenly on the people of the village, who fled when they saw us, men and women alike. The Indian I had with me reassured them and told them not to be afraid, for we were good people. I told the men to give them some little bells and brass rings and green and yellow glass beads, with which they were very pleased... (*Columbus' Journal,* translated by John Cummins, Monday, December 3, 1492).

The Indian accompanying my men ran after them shouting to them to have no fear, for my men were not from Caniba, but from Heaven, and were giving away many fine things to everyone they came across. What he said impressed them so much that over two thousand of them came back, and they all kept coming up to put their hands on my men's heads as a sign of great reverence and friendship (*Columbus' Journal,* translated by John Cummins, Thursday, December 13, 1492).

Revisionists highlight the "kidnapping" part of the story but fail to tell us the reason why he was doing it, or that in the end, he earned their trust.

The Indian went ashore in his canoe and told the villagers that we were good people, though they already knew this from what happened in the other villages visited by my six men (*Columbus' Journal,* translated by John Cummins, Sunday, December 16, 1492).

At sunrise the king came to tell me that he had sent for gold and that before I leave he will cover me in it. He begged me to stay; he and his brother and another close relative ate with me, and these last two told me that they wished to come to Castile with me (*Columbus' Journal,* translated by John Cummins, Thursday, December 27, 1492).

Revisionists won't mention that Columbus returned the natives and paid them for the trouble. What I find more fascinating is that the Queen of Spain, whose maternal heart felt for the natives and asked Columbus to treat them with kindness, never complained or said anything against it. Perhaps it's because the queen saw it as an essential part of the conquest. Yet, revisionists won't say one word when it was the natives kidnapping one another for war or cannibalistic raids.

3. Heavy Tribute- Another thing that could be considered as an argument of constructive criticism is the fact that Columbus imposed a heavy tribute upon the natives of Hispaniola. That's one of the reasons why Columbus reduced the gold quota to half; a detail skipped by revisionists, as stated in previous chapters.

Revisionists didn't have to lie about Columbus to find out his sins and mistakes. Yet, as bad as they were, they have nothing to do with the memes and false templates we see everywhere today on the web and in the media. They have nothing to do with racism, hate, fictional child sex slavery rings, genocide, conspiratorial spreading of deadly diseases to wipe out enemy countries, or any other imaginary crime.

4. Giving women away- This is the part where revisionists claim Columbus was giving native women away to the Spaniards to get raped. Of course, that charge is ridiculous! In his own words, Columbus "gave women away" once, to both Spaniards AND native men, during his first voyage. However, he was not the inventor of such a custom. Columbus explained:

I did this because men behave better in Spain when they have women of their own land with them than when they are <u>deprived</u> of them.

That's why I wrote Columbus "gave women away" in quotation marks; because it is not that he gave them away, but that he would not deprive his men, or the native men he took with him, from women. Columbus, who had lived in Portugal for several years, explained what the Portuguese used to do:

<u>Men have often been taken from Guinea to Portugal to learn the language</u>, and given good treatment and gifts, and when they were taken back with a view to employing them in their own country they went ashore and were never seen again. Others behaved differently.

This is where Columbus probably got the idea of kidnapping, which it shows that he was doing what others used to do before him. Columbus continued:

If they have their women they will be eager to take on whatever duties one asks of them, and the women themselves will be good for teaching our people their language, which is the same throughout all these islands of India. They all understand each other, and go about from island to island in their canoes; quite differently from in Guinea, where there are a thousand different languages, incomprehensible to one another (*Columbus' Journal*, translated by John Cummins, Monday, November 12, 1492).

Notice that Columbus never said anything about rape there. However, since I am a Christian, my opinion is the same as primary historical source and priest, Bartolomé de las Casas. He criticized Columbus for making "fine excuses" for sin and condemned these actions as adultery, **IF** the natives he took with him were already married, or perhaps incest, **IF** the natives were family related with one another. Las Casas was just speculating about the natives' marital status, yet he didn't say anything about rape. See *Historia de las Indias* by Las Casas, Tomo I, Lib. I, Cap. XLVI, p. 336.

Columbus wasn't "giving women away" 24/7 as revisionists want us to believe. The only time he did this was the one time mentioned above, on the 12th of November 1492 journal entry of his first voyage. That was all for that excursion. There is no evidence that he kept doing this during the rest of the voyage. In fact, almost two months later, Columbus was upset with one of the Pinzón brothers saying:

> When he left here he took away four Indians and two girls by force. I have ordered them to be given clothes and taken ashore so that they may go home. Treating them thus can only be to Your Majesties' benefit, in all the islands but especially in this one, where you now have a settlement, for in an island with such a wealth of gold and spices and fine land the people must be treated honourably and generously (*Columbus' Journal*, translated by John Cummins, Thursday, January 10, 1493).

The lesson we can learn from this episode of Columbus is that, as Christians, we should not participate in sin, even if it is culturally accepted. Otherwise, the actions will backfire on us, just as it happened with Columbus. Las Casas said:

A sin might seem like nothing to us, or that it won't harm us much, because of our blindness or habit, or availability to sin, or because of the good that sometimes comes from it; but before God, sin is judged as something very serious and very grave, and our flesh should tremble if we were to reach such consideration (*Historia de las Indias* by Las Casas, Tomo I, Lib. I, Cap. XLVI, p. 337. Translation from Spanish to English is mine).

Now, did you know some native tribes used to give their women away too? In fact, it was a custom for some tribes. Worse, at one time they sent two minors, during Columbus' fourth voyage, while they were trading with them. The natives told them "to take the girls." Ferdinand's account, which is aimed for public audiences, says the girls were eight and fourteen years of age. But Columbus' letter, which was for the king and queen's eyes only, says one was seven and the other eleven years old. Columbus was upset with the situation and said that both girls were "behaving with such lack of modesty as to be no better than whores." The Spanish word he used for "whores," is an expletive in modern Spanish language. It doesn't mean that Columbus was cursing, since he was not given to profanity. It just means the word is explicit in today's Spanish.

Where are the revisionists condemning such actions? Where is the outrage against natives? And why would Columbus be upset with the natives sending him minors if he was a pedophile and a rapist?

So, how did Columbus respond? Columbus "clothed and fed" them, "and then sent them ashore." Giving clothes away as gifts was something Columbus did in all of his voyages, especially to women. See *Columbus's Lettera Rarissima to the Sovereigns*, from *Journal and Other Documents* by Morison, p. 381, and *The*

Life of the Admiral Christopher Columbus by his son Ferdinand, Ch. 91, p. 237.

In addition, the natives gave their women away to subsequent explorers, including Amerigo Vespucci, Hernán Cortés, Ferdinand Magellan, Hernando de Soto, etc. [2]

Any outrage against the natives for doing what Columbus did once? Or is the outrage exclusively reserved for Columbus?

So, where do these false rape allegations come from? It came from a Columbus' friend, named Michele de Cuneo, who accompanied him during his second voyage to the New World.

Chapter 30. Michele de Cuneo

According to a letter Cuneo wrote to a friend, he admitted to raping a native girl that was supposedly given to him by Columbus. Revisionists love Michele de Cuneo's rape story because in their view, Columbus is guilty by association. This Cuneo's rape story is in many of Columbus' biographies out there, as if Cuneo was Columbus himself, or his clone, or as if Columbus knew what his friend did and approved or applauded the assault!

Columbus wasn't in the bedroom with his friend to know what he did. The reason why we know today Cuneo's rape story is because he wrote about it in a personal letter that became public **centuries** later in 1885. This is assuming the letter is authentic in its entirety, since some scholars challenged it in the past due to "inconsistencies in style." [1] Today it is accepted as genuine because it passed the test of paleography in the 19th-century. The original letter doesn't exist and what we have today is a copy made around 1511. Of course, that doesn't mean it's a fake, but it doesn't mean it's all true either. The fact is since Columbus became famous many forged letters, or authentic ones containing false information, have come to surface.

So let's look at some of the inconsistencies and falsehoods in Cuneo's letter:

He started the letter with, "In the name of Jesus and of His Glorious Mother Mary," but a few pages later he rapes a native girl. Cuneo seems to contradict himself as well when he said, "While I was in the boat I captured a very beautiful Carib woman, whom the said Lord Admiral gave to me." Which is true? That Cuneo "captured" her, or that the Lord Admiral "gave" her to him?

Cuneo claimed he took the Carib girl he raped to his cabin, where she screamed at the top of her lungs after he beat her for initially denying him intercourse. [2] If that is so, how come no one else heard the screaming? Can you imagine the enemies of Columbus if they had heard a native woman screaming because Columbus gave her away to be raped? Columbus' enemies would have had a field day with such an accusation!

Another falsehood by Cuneo is the existence of temples in the Caribbean, when there were none.

Cuneo is also the only "source" claiming Columbus was in love with a woman named Beatriz de Bobadilla (or de Peraza). She was the Countess of La Gomera island, in the Canary Islands when Columbus stopped there to supply his ships with water and food.

There were also two respectable persons who were in the same second voyage when the alleged rape happened. One was a doctor named Doctor Diego Álvarez Chanca, and the other was Guillermo Coma of Aragon. Neither Dr. Chanca, Guillermo Coma, and I would add Ferdinand Columbus, Peter Martyr, Las Casas, Herrera, or any other credible source ever mentioned that Columbus was in love with Beatriz de Bobadilla, or that Columbus was raping or giving women away to be raped. [3]

Cuneo also said that when the native girl yielded to him, "she seemed to have been brought up in a school of harlots." That means Cuneo knew what such a "school" would be like. So here we are taking the words of a cheater, a gossip and a rapist as "gospel."

During this second voyage, Columbus kept the Spaniards from native women. If Columbus let Cuneo keep a native girl, it was because he was not a Spaniard and he expected better behavior from Cuneo as a friend.

Strangely enough, those who hated Columbus, accused him of everything, except giving women away to be raped. In fact, one of the complaints against Columbus and his brothers by Roldán and his rebels (during the third voyage) was that they "made them observe the three monastic vows;" that is poverty, **chastity**, and obedience. [4]

Columbus sent letters to the Spanish kings reporting that Roldán and his accomplices were harassing the native women. See *Historia de las Indias* by Las Casas, Tomo II, Lib. I, Cap. CLIX, pp. 360-361.

That was the timeline when Columbus called these Spanish rebels, "**debauchees, profligates,** thieves, **seducers, ravishers,** vagabonds," etc. *De Orbe Novo* by Peter Martyr, The First Decade, Book VII, p. 142.

"Debauchees" means "a person addicted to excessive indulgence in **sensual pleasures**; one given to debauchery." The word "profligate" means "utterly and shamelessly **immoral** or dissipated; thoroughly dissolute." "Ravisher" means "**rapist**." [5]

It is clear Columbus wasn't pleased with the Spaniards, and he wasn't giving them women as he did once. It's also clear Columbus was not okay with rape.

It is ironic how revisionists highlighted, and magnified Michele de Cuneo's rape story, but avoided the parts **in the very same letter** where he confirmed that the Caribs depopulated islands with raids, slavery, rapes, murder, and cannibalism. Cuneo also tells us that, in the meantime, Columbus was rescuing the Taínos from being kidnapped and raped by the Caribs. This is what he wrote:

In that island we took twelve very beautiful and very
fat women from 15 to 16 years old, together with two
boys of the same age. These had the genital organ
cut to the belly; and this we thought had been done
in order to prevent them from meddling with their
wives or maybe to fatten them up and later eat
them... there were three or four Carib men with two
Carib women and two Indian **slaves**, of whom (that
is the way the Caribs treat their other neighbors in
those other islands), they had recently cut the
genital organ to the belly, so that they were still
sore. [6]

Where is the outrage against these kidnappings and
castrations? Guillermo Coma, who was on the same voyage as
Cuneo, confirmed the rape raids by the Caribs in a letter:

They hand over the female captives as slaves to
their womenfolk, or make use of them to satisfy
their **lust**. Children borne by the captured women
are eaten like the captives. [7]

Any outrage against this? Why is that some websites are so
willing to stain Columbus' reputation with innuendos, by using
selected portions of Cuneo's letter, but skip the parts where Cuneo reported the natives were doing the same things revisionists
pretend they lament?

In addition, Cuneo's description of the natives was not
positive either. He said the natives ate poisonous beasts, insects,
reptiles, dogs, snakes, lizards, spiders, etc. According to him, the
natives would cut their own father's head off and then cook it, as
told by their idols, if the father was sick with no hope to re-
cuperate. The first woman to enter their temple would have sex

with their "holy man." They would have sex anywhere openly, with anyone, except with brothers and sisters; they were sodomites; they were cold-blooded people; they would live short lives, etc. [8]

Should we take that as "gospel" too? In fact, the description of the natives above is another reason why I've been skeptical of Cuneo's account. Whereas every primary source made distinction from Caribs and Taínos, Cuneo painted them all with the same broad brush. Also, the charge of sodomy came many years later after Columbus was dead, yet here we have Cuneo making the claim supposedly in 1495. Sodomy was the worst sin you could charge someone with during this period of time. It's interesting that neither Columbus nor any other primary source said anything about the matter, which they would if they had seen it.

In spite of all these objections, Cuneo's letter could still be authentic. For example, the conflict of words when he said he "captured" the girl vs. Columbus "gave" her to him, could be a mistranslation or it could be the way Cuneo spoke. The "temples" in the Caribbean could be a reference to the huts the natives used for religious purposes. Columbus "being in love" with the Countess of La Gomera could be just pure gossip. The native sexual immorality could be an exaggeration or/and a generalization.

Samuel Eliot Morison, who translated Cuneo's letter into English says Cuneo was not like Columbus or the "solem Spaniards who wrote on the early voyages." Morison admitted Cuneo's narrative is "somewhat confused." Cuneo did not care if he was really in the east or if Columbus' discovery was foretold by Scriptures. Cuneo was there just to have "fun," and that is what he did.

Anyone reading Columbus' accounts can clearly see that Columbus was very protective toward the native women. It is also clear that the rapists in Cuneo's account, by his own admission, were him and the Caribs, and not Columbus.

Chapter 31. Bartolomé de las Casas

Las Casas, or his full name, Bartolomé de las Casas, was a contemporary of Columbus and a primary historical source used in this book. He wrote several books, including *Historia de las Indias,* which are three (or more) lengthy volumes, and only available today in an archaic Spanish language. The only English version available (*History of the Indies*) is a 292 page long edited summary version of the lengthy originals, and it does not do any justice to Columbus' story.

Las Casas was a Christian priest and a historian. He, along with other clerics, fought for the rights and freedom of the natives, centuries before Lincoln and the abolishment movement ever existed. He wrote about the Spaniards' mistreatment of the natives in *A Brief Account of the Destruction of the Indies* book, which is available in contemporary English today, sometimes under a different title, like *A Short Account...* or *Tears of the Indians,* etc. The book is infuriating to read as it describes the abuses some Spaniards imposed onto the natives. But both, *A Brief Account* and *History of the Indies,* have been often misquoted by revisionists attributing the Spaniards' atrocities to Columbus.

An example of it is a YouTube video where Hollywood actor Viggo Mortensen reads selected portions of Las Casas' *A Brief Account of the Destruction of the Indies.* [1] The problem is that the events of the book happened AFTER Columbus was out of office. The beginning of *A Brief Account* clearly states that, "the desolation of these Isles and Provinces **took beginning** since the decease of the most Serene Queen Isabella, **about the year 1504**, for **before that time very few** of the Provinces situated in that Island were oppressed or spoiled with **unjust wars...**"

Columbus was out of office in 1500 and he died in 1506. Not only that, but many of the places where the atrocities took place in that book, were places Columbus never visited, including Mexico, Guatemala, Bogotá, Perú and Florida. The others were places Columbus visited, but never settled, including San Juan island (Puerto Rico), Nicaragua, Trinidad, Cuba and Venezuela. Hispaniola was the only place where Columbus was directly involved, specifically arresting Caonabó, which Las Casas lamented, but he did not explain why he was arrested. The years used in the book for the atrocities were 1504, 1506, 1514, 1522, 1542, etc. Again, years after Columbus out of the scene.

Some time ago I caught someone on social media posting some excerpts from *A Brief Account* with Columbus' name at the bottom of the quote. In other words, this person signed Columbus' name to manipulate the context, implying Columbus was the one making the statement and the atrocities were committed by him. This person blocked me after I respectfully confronted him with the truth.

Contrary to what some people may think, Las Casas was not a "pacifist" either. Las Casas' criticism against Columbus, in relation to the natives, was not because he was an anti-war activist, or against enslaving war defeated foes. Las Casas criticized Columbus because he believed he and the Spaniards were carrying on an **unjust war** against the natives. That would mean Las Casas would not have minded the war and the enslavement of enemy combatants if the war were "just" in Las Casas' estimation.

As a Catholic priest, Las Casas believed in St. Augustine's "Just War Theory" and Thomas Aquinas' "Natural Law" philosophy. That's why he constantly spoke of "just," "unjust war" and "Natural Law" in his books. In fact, in many places in his writings he said the natives had **just cause** for killing Spaniards. Remember, the Bible says there is "a time for war and a time for peace." Ecclesiastes 3:8 (NIV). "Even beasts are allowed the right of self-defense," Las Casas wrote (*History of the Indies*, Book Two, Ch. 19, p. 129).

However, Las Casas' overzeal for the natives caused him to overlook certain things and misjudge Columbus in others. Further, he made many false claims, unintended contradictions, and exaggerations, that even some scholars who don't like Columbus have to admit he did. Here are some examples:

He would romanticize the natives as almost sinless and peaceful people, which is absurd and preposterous. Even though it is true that many natives, in the Caribbean, were kind, gentle, and generous, they were not as peaceful as Las Casas claimed in his books. The natives of the smaller islands were timid and frequently attacked by cannibals, while the natives on the bigger islands, like Cuba and Hispaniola, were in a constant war.

Notice how Peter Martyr praised the natives for their generosity, while at the same time he acknowledged they were in constant war and strife with each other:

> They go naked, they know neither weights nor measures, nor that source of all misfortunes, money; living in a golden age, without laws, without lying judges, without books, satisfied with their life, and in no wise solicitous for the future. Nevertheless ambition and the desire to rule trouble even them, and **they fight amongst themselves, so that even in the golden age there is never a moment without war**... (*De Orbe Novo* by Peter Martyr, The First Decade, Book II, p. 79).

Hispaniola:

The natives are **ferocious and warlike**, and it is thought they are of the same race as the cannibals, for when they descend from their mountains to fight with their neighbours in the plain, they eat all whom they kill (*De Orbe Novo* by Peter Martyr, The First Decade, Book V, p. 127).

In Jamaica:

... to the left of Cuba, an island called by the natives Jamaica... According to the report of their neighbours, the natives of this island have a keener intelligence and are cleverer in mechanical arts, as well as **more warlike than others**. And indeed, each time the Admiral [Columbus] sought to land in any place, they assembled in armed bands, threatening him, and not hesitating to offer battle (*De Orbe Novo* by Peter Martyr, The First Decade, Book III, p. 93).

In Cuba:

[Years later after Columbus' death, the natives of Cuba were described as] **often** at war one with another (*De Orbe Novo* by Peter Martyr, The Second Decade, Book VI, p. 241).

In the mainland:

These caciques rob and massacre one another, and destroy their villages, during their atrocious wars. They give no quarter, and the victors make a clean sweep of everything (*De Orbe Novo* by Peter Martyr, The Third Decade, Book X, p. 406).

Las Casas was correct that the natives had the right to defend themselves against the Spaniards' abuses, but Columbus had the same right to defend himself against the attacks of Caonabó, especially since Columbus had nothing to do with the Spaniards' abuses and he did everything he could to keep the peace between both groups. Columbus was not the Spaniards, and the Spaniards were not on the same page with Columbus. Let's not confuse the two.

When Columbus forgave the natives that were sentenced to death (in Chapter 17), Las Casas commented:

Reason itself says it was not right to trespass, not right to do it in a warlike manner, and not right that the admiral leave the ship without first sending an embassy to notify the Indian kings of his intention to visit them, asking permission to do so and sending gifts, as he was instructed to do by the King of Castile. The admiral should have taken pains to bring love and peace and to avoid scandalous incidents, for not to perturb the innocent is a precept of evangelical law whose messenger he was."
History of the Indies by Las Casas, Book One, Ch. 93, pp. 52-53.

"Evangelical law" also says that Columbus, as a government authority, did have the right to impart justice. The Bible says, "rulers do not bear the sword for no reason. They are God's

198

servants, agents of wrath to bring punishment on the wrong-doer." Romans 13:4 (NIV). That was also the timeline where Columbus was in constant harassment and death threatened by Caonabó, which is why he entered in a "warlike manner... in order to show the Indians that they could not do to him what they had done" to the 39 Spaniards (*The Life of the Admiral Christopher Columbus* by his son Ferdinand, Ch. 51, p. 123).

I don't know how Las Casas missed that. At least Las Casas said in the next paragraph that "truly, I would not dare blame the admiral's intention, **for I knew him well and all I know his intentions were good**" (*History of the Indies* by Las Casas, Book One, Ch. 93, p. 53).

Las Casas also would not believe Columbus' sincerity when he said that even though he sold some natives as slaves, he intended to return them back to freedom in Hispaniola (*History of the Indies* by Las Casas, Book Two, Ch. 37, p. 141).

When Columbus wrote "I should be judged as a captain who left Spain for the Indies to conquer a warlike nation," Las Casas had a footnote which sarcastically said, Columbus "did not call it warlike when Guacanagarí saved his life when his ship sank" (*History of the Indies* by Las Casas, Book One, Ch. 181, p. 75).

Guacanagarí didn't save Columbus' life, and Guacanagarí was in peace terms with Columbus What does one thing have to do with the other? And don't forget that Caonabó later "stole" (kidnapped) one of Guacanagarí's wives, while cacique Behecio killed another (*The Life of the Admiral Christopher Columbus* by his son Ferdinand, Ch. 61, p. 148).

When Columbus made the natives pay tribute, Las Casas said that it was an "impossible" task (*Historia de las Indias*, Tomo II, Lib. I, Cap. CV, p. 104). If the tribute were literally "impossible," Columbus would have never demanded it. But since it was very hard, he decided to cut the quota in half.

During Columbus' fourth voyage, Columbus imprisoned a chief because he had found out he was planning to kill him. Las Casas asked, "what authority had he to enslave <u>that whole tribe</u> when, in a state of servitude, that tribe was equal, perhaps even superior, to the Spaniards as free men, except in matters of Faith and Christianity?" (*History of the Indies* by Las Casas, Book Two, Ch. 27, p. 130). That's another exaggeration by Las Casas. Columbus didn't enslave the whole tribe. He "enslaved," or took hostage the chief, his family, and other "leading Indians" because Columbus and his men were outnumbered in fighting a whole tribe of natives. And again, Columbus, or really his brother, did this because they found out the chief was plotting to kill them all (*The Life of the Admiral Christopher Columbus* by his son Ferdinand, Ch. 97, pp. 256-257).

As for the question, under "what authority" Columbus was doing this? The answer to Las Casas would be, the authority of self-defense, which Las Casas many times advocated for, when it was the natives defending themselves from the Spaniards' abuses. Las Casas called it, "Natural Law." Moreover, the authority Columbus had as a leader came from the Queen of Spain herself, who Las Casas idolized so much. Lastly, Columbus had the authority of the Spanish kingdom, whom he was owed the title of viceroy of all the lands discovered by him.

One of the very few times revisionists quote Las Casas accurately was when he falsely claimed Columbus was responsible for the depopulation of a third of Hispaniola from 1494 to 1496. As we have seen in Chapter 20, most people died due to a famine provoked by the natives themselves. Yet, Las Casas added the number of natives who died in war to the death toll. Ironically, Las Casas proceeded to make some harsh allegations against Columbus that revisionists could have used, but instead they chose to make things up about Columbus.

Las Casas claimed that after Caonabó was arrested, Columbus went on a military tour for nine or ten months killing natives "without cause or reason," "especially in Caonabó's kingdom, being his brothers braves" ("en especial en el reino de Caonabo, por ser sus hermanos tan valientes." *Historia de las Indias*, Tomo II, Lib. I, Cap. CV, p. 101).

According to Las Casas, Columbus went to kill anyone who opposed him, depopulating towns, where people were cut in half with swords, torn and eaten by dogs, and many were burned alive. He claimed infinite numbers of people died. Las Casas claimed he got all this information by reading the letters Columbus sent to the Spanish crown.

If what Las Casas claimed was true (that Columbus was killing infinite numbers of people for no reason), and writing about it to the king and queen, Columbus would have been in big trouble with them. But Las Casas' claims are false and distorted.

When Las Casas said Columbus was killing "without cause or reason," he meant that Columbus did not have a "just cause" in his estimate. Though we don't have the letters Las Casas reported he had read, we do have Peter Martyr's account explaining what happened:

After Columbus made the natives pay tribute, Caonabó asked him for his assistance to help him fight his enemies. This was mentioned in a quote in Chapter 23 of this book. However, Caonabó's plea was a trap. Columbus consented to Caonabó's request and sent Hojeda to the region, but they were ambushed by Caonabó's brother with an Indigenous army of 5,000 men. Luckily, Hojeda defeated them in the battle and then there was peace. Is that killing people "without cause or reason"? Swords and dogs were the Spaniards' weapons, and of course, weapons kill people. Do you see how off Las Casas was?

Let's keep exploring Las Casas' war death toll, not only until 1496, but afterwards:

After Columbus departed for Spain in 1496, he left his brother Bartholomew in charge of the island during his absence. During this time, two chiefs convinced Chief Guarionex to rebel and attack Bartholomew Columbus. They were planning to raise an Indigenous army of 15,000, but Bartholomew discovered the conspiracy and made a surprise attack winning the victory. Bartholomew condemned to death only the chiefs who conspired against him, but he gave Guarionex a second chance in an attempt to win him as an ally. The problem was that Roldán and his Spanish mutineers started their rebellion against Bartholomew during this timeline, and went to harass the natives, as they did many times in disobedience of Spanish law. This gave Guarionex an excuse to stop paying tribute and to flee to some other chief's land for protection. Bartholomew confronted Roldán, but he fled with his men to another town before Bartholomew could arrest them. There, he and the mutineers brought more trouble to the natives. Meanwhile, Guarionex assembled an army of natives and they frequently attacked and killed Spaniards and their Indigenous allies, destroying their villages.

When Columbus returned to Hispaniola in 1498, he sent his brother Bartholomew to fight Guarionex with 90 foot soldiers, some horsemen, but also with 3,000 natives who were victims of Guarionex and the Ciguana tribe. See Chapter 23. There were a few skirmishes, but in order to win the peace, Bartholomew Columbus sent a native messenger to the chief who was hosting Guarionex, to give him up in exchange for peace and alliance. The chief declined the offer, so Bartholomew burned a few villages as a threat to the chief of what would happen to him if he would not give up Guarionex. There is no evidence people were in those villages, since earlier they have fled due to the war between these two opponents. The chief refused again to concede to Bartholomew's request and decapitated Bartholomew's messengers.

Eventually, the chief was captured and Guarionex gave himself up. See *De Orbe Novo*, The First Decade, Book V, pp. 121-149.

Do you see how much of the story was left out by Las Casas? Note that Las Casas did not condemn Caonabó for burning Guacanagarí's village for hosting the 39 men Columbus left there during the first voyage, and he did not condemn Chief Guatiganá for ordering to set on fire the hut where 40 sick men were lodged during the second voyage. Nor did he condemn another chief who tried to burn the Spanish settlement in the continent during Columbus' fourth voyage.

Likewise, Las Casas neither criticized the queen for the Inquisition, nor did he call the battle against the Moors in Granada an "unjust war." He did not criticize Spain for enslaving Moorish enemy combatants either. If you wonder why Las Casas believed all wars against the natives were "unjust," it was because he believed the natives would go to hell for not knowing the true God. But even that claim is not entirely true since many natives had converted to Christianity and sometimes joined the Spaniards to fight other tribes.

At a time when conquest was the rule of the day, Las Casas did have a lot of legitimate and logical questions against it.

> He combated the almost universally accepted theory that justifiable conquest conferred the right of enslaving the conquered, and he maintained that the most that might be exacted from a conquered people, even from those who had actively resisted, was recognition of the government established by the victorious party; taxes were justifiable and must be paid, and prisoners of war might be held until the close of hostilities, while extra burdens might be laid upon the country during the period of military occupation. Not one of these principles was at that

time acted upon by any Christian power engaged in war with uncivilised nations, yet every one of them is now placed beyond dispute by the universally accepted principles of international law. [2]

However, Las Casas still believed in conquest, but by persuasion.

Reduced to a formula the doctrine of Las Casas may be summed up: Convert the Indians first and they will afterwards become Spanish subjects; as against the contention of his adversaries that they must first be conquered, after which their conversion would follow. [3]

Again, politics back then were different from today. When it comes to slavery, Las Casas was not against it in the beginning, but instead, he was against the mistreatment of the slaves. He even suggested bringing African slaves to help the natives in their labor! (*History of the Indies* by Las Casas, Book Three, Ch. 129, p. 257).

We need to remember that slavery was normal back then, practiced in every continent, and it was part of how the economic system worked. His fellow priests owned slaves as well, until they saw how the colonists were mistreating them. Then, they started to denounce the slavery system as a mortal sin. Initially, Las Casas did not agree with his fellow Dominican friars, but he later repented realizing that slavery, and not just the mistreatment of the slaves, was wrong. Once Las Casas' eyes were opened, he had to give up his own slaves (yes, he owned slaves too) before he could preach against it (*History of the Indies* by Las Casas, Book Three, Ch. 79, pp. 208-209).

Las Casas, along with some of his fellow clerics, suffered a lot of resistance, because giving up slavery, meant society had to figure out another way to do economics without them. It's easy to criticize the people of the past and judge them, but I want to remind you, the reader, that if you were living back in those days, you might be doing the exact same things everyone else was doing back then. You might be conquering or being conquered; enslaving or being enslaved. That's why we should look at history with **humility**, and not with contempt, and give thanks to God that we are not living that way today. On the other hand, revisionists see history with contempt and guilt... white guilt.

Las Casas condemned Columbus for selling natives as slaves, yet he still said that Columbus was doing it out of "blindness" and "ignorance," and not because Columbus was an evil man. Not to mention that slavery was sanctioned by the Spanish monarchs, who followed the opinions of the learned men of their day. That's why Las Casas said that if those who the "sovereigns had for eyes and light, were so ignorant of the injustice of this practice, it is no wonder that the admiral should be ignorant of it, who was not a learned man" (*Historia de las Indias*, Tomo II, Lib. I, Cap. CXXII, p. 177).

Las Casas also believed that the many trials Columbus suffered were God's judgment for Columbus' "unjust war" on the natives. "It is not too bold," Las Casas wrote, "to presume that his anguish and misfortune were sent as divine punishment..." *History of the Indies*, Book Two, Ch. 38, p. 144.

Columbus was a man of his time, while Las Casas became a man ahead of his time. Some people have suggested we should rename Columbus Day to "Bartolomé de las Casas Day." Laurence Bergreen concluded his Columbus book, *The Four Voyages,* with an Epilogue titled "Columbus Day," where he said that the "most lasting damage to Columbus's reputation came from the pen of" Bartolomé de las Casas. [4] However, Bergreen's assessment lacks the context I just gave above.

Even though it is true that Las Casas denounced Columbus for a handful of "unjust wars" and "unjust" slavery, he also defended Columbus' honor and dignity. As John Cummins said, "There is something of this even in the work of Las Casas, a great and scholarly defender of both **the reputation of Columbus** and the rights of the Indians." [5]

Those who suggest renaming Columbus Day, to "Bartolomé de las Casas Day" don't know what they are talking about, because if Las Casas were alive today, he would be the first one to protest such foolishness. Remember, he was not pleased that the continent was named after Amerigo Vespucci. What's more, though Las Casas scolded Columbus for a few things (some fair, while others very unfair), it was also he who defended him, and had countless good things to say about him.

To those who like to quote Las Casas condemning Columbus, without providing context, I will quote to you some of the things Las Casas said about Columbus, in context, in his defense, from his *History of the Indies* translated and edited by Andrée M. Collard. Las Casas described Columbus as:

> ... imposing, good natured, kind, daring, courageous, and a pious man... God had endowed him with good judgment, a sound memory and eagerness to learn... as a God fearing man... he must have avoided exaggeration. *p. 15.*

> **I think Christopher Columbus was the most outstanding sailor in the world**, versed like no other in the art of navigation, for which divine Providence chose him to accomplish the most outstanding feat ever accomplished in the world until now. *p. 17.*

> Christopher Columbus, to whom all Christendom is so greatly indebted. *p. 18.*

... he was well-mannered, handsome man and a church-going Christian... *p. 19.*

.. well spoken, wise and prudent. *p. 29.*

The excellence of Columbus's project and its inestimable value... *p 30.*

Many is the time I have wished that God would again inspire me and that I had Cicero's gift of eloquence to extol the **indescribable service to God and to the whole world** which Christopher Columbus **rendered at the cost of such pain and dangers**, such skill and expertise, when he so **courageously discovered** the New World. *pp. 34-35.*

My limited understanding and poor eloquence prompt me to think that the fruit of Columbus's labor speaks better for itself than I do... **God gave this man the keys to the awesome seas, he and no other unlocked the darkness, to him and to no other is owed for ever** and ever all that exists beyond those doors. *p. 35.*

Wow! I wonder what revisionists would think while reading all this!

It is fitting to stress that **God** most sublimely favored all of Spain over other Christian nation, when he **chose** Christopher Columbus to give to Spain such a golden opportunity in every sense of the word. *p. 36.*

... that **most worthy man** Christopher **Columbus was the cause**, second to God but first in the eyes of men, being **the discoverer and only worthy first admiral of the vast territory known as the New World**... *p. 37.*

Las Casas called Columbus a <u>hero</u> when he returned to Spain from his first voyage:

The streets were crammed with people... all of them beaming with happiness and anxious to greet **the hero** of the exploit... *p. 38.*

What more universal pleasure had ever affected the whole Christian world, a pleasure which, surely, was caused by God's acceptance of the discovery? *p. 39.*

... it is clear that **Columbus discovered the continent**... Which should have been called Columba and not as it is unjustly called, America. *p. 62.*

Honor and titles he **well deserved and well earned**, for no services so famous were ever rendered to any other earthly King... **he is owed the praise**. *pp. 134-135.*

Las Casas also described Columbus as a sensitive man:

[The] news that Queen Isabella had died filled Columbus with intense grief. To him, she represented protection and hope, and no amount of pain, hardship or loss (even loss of his own life) could afflict and sadden him more than such news. *p. 138.*

The King received them [Columbus and his brothers], graciously, although not as graciously as their long peregrinations, hardships and experience **deserved**. *p. 139.*

... his exploits so unjustly forgotten... *p. 143.*

... he was a good Christian... *p. 143.*

"He was a good Christian" was the last description Las Casas gave when Columbus died. Through all his books, Las Casas always described Columbus as a good man, with good intentions.

Chapter 32. Washington Irving vs. The

Myth Makers

Who was Washington Irving, and what did he have to do with Christopher Columbus? Washington Irving was the famous 19th-century writer of *The Legend of Sleepy Hollow,* whose character has appeared in many TV shows and Hollywood movies, one version starring Johnny Depp. Irving also wrote one of the most popular biographies of Columbus titled, *A History of the Life and Voyages of Christopher Columbus,* which modern revisionists attack as a work of "fiction" and "hero myth-making."

Revisionists dismiss Irving as "just a fiction writer," even though he also wrote nonfiction and historical books like *The Adventures of Captain Bonneville, Astoria, Chronicle of the Conquest of Granada, Life of Oliver Goldsmith* and a biography of George Washington, whom he was named after.

Benjamin Keen, the translator of *The Life of the Admiral Christopher Columbus by his son Ferdinand,* wrote in the introduction that "Irving had access to a wealth of sources... but... in what Kirkpatrick Sale rightly calls 'a glaring abdication of the responsibility of the historian in favor of the license of the novelist,' he 'created an essentially **fictional hero** for whose actions it was not necessary to provide documentation...' "

What? A "fictional hero"? Was George Washington a "fictional hero" too? Is George Washington's biography a work of fiction? After all, Irving was a "mythmaker," right? The complaint is exclusive to Columbus. I wonder why? I think his critics are just jealous of Irving's success, especially since none of their works have become as popular as Irving's.

Keen continued: "Irving consistently omits or glosses over the darker sides of Columbus's life, especially his conduct toward the Indians. And, as we have already noted, he readily accepts the most spurious legends about Columbus, including the legend that Columbus's opponents believed the world was flat, the anecdote of the egg, and the story that Isabella offered to pawn her jewels to finance his enterprise." [1]

Interestingly, Benjamin Keen's book quotes Washington Irving on the back cover, and not Kirkpatrick Sale, or any other Columbus detractors, to promote his Ferdinand Columbus translation. The Irving quote on the back cover says the following: "The cornerstone of the history of the American continent." Question: Is that quote fictional too? A myth? Why use a quote by a "myth maker" to promote Keen's translated book, and not a more "credible" source instead? I wonder if Keen and other Irving critics ever read Irving's biography of Columbus, because most of their charges against Irving are false!

First of all, Columbus is not a "fictional hero," but a hero of historic proportions. Irving didn't create any myth. Revisionists do. Revisionists are also the ones who usually don't provide documentation to prove their "Columbus was evil" myth.

Secondly, Irving "had access to a wealth of sources," and he certainly used them all. His biography of Columbus was not one or two books, but three, and sometimes released in four volumes, depending on the publishing house. Every chapter includes quotes or footnotes from primary historical sources and documentation.

Third, Irving did not omit or gloss over "the darker sides of Columbus's life." Columbus didn't have any. If by "his conduct toward the Indians," Mr. Keen means slavery, then he is wrong again. This is what Irving had to say about the subject:

> It is painful to find the brilliant renown of Columbus sullied by so foul a stain, and the glory of his enterprizes degraded by such flagrant violations of human right.

Perhaps what revisionists don't like is what Irving said next:

> The customs of the times, however, must be pleaded in his apology. The precedent had been given long before, by both Spaniards and Portuguese, in their African discoveries, wherein the traffic in slaves had formed one of the greatest sources of profit. In fact, the practice had been sanctioned by the highest authority; by that of the church itself; and the most learned theologians had pronounced all barbarous and infidel nations, who shut their ears to the truths of Christianity, as fair objects of war and rapine, of captivity and slavery. If Columbus needed any practical illustration of this doctrine, he had it in the conduct of Ferdinand himself, in his late wars with the Moors of Granada, in which he had always been surrounded by a cloud of ghostly advisers, and had professed to do everything for the glory and advancement of the faith. In this holy war, as it was termed, it was a common practice to make inroads into the Moorish territories and carry off *cavalgadas*, not merely of flocks and herds, but of human beings, and those, not warriors taken with weapons in their hands, but quiet villagers, labouring peasantry, and helpless

women and children (*A History of the Life and Voyages of Christopher Columbus* by Washington Irving, Vol. 2, Book VIII, Ch. V, p. 85).

True also to the times, Muslims were doing the same, and so were the natives. In another chapter, Irving stated:

[Columbus] considered himself justified in making captives of the Indians, and transporting them to Spain to have them taught the doctrines of Christianity, and in selling them for slaves, if they pretended to resist his invasions. In doing the latter **he sinned** against the natural benignity of his character, and against the feelings which he had originally entertained and expressed towards this gentle and hospitable people; but he was goaded on by the mercenary impatience of the crown, and by the sneers of his enemies at the unprofitable result of his enterprizes. It is but justice to his character to observe, that the enslavement of the Indians thus taken in battle was at first openly countenanced by the crown, and that when the question of right came to be discussed at the instance of the queen, several of the most distinguished jurists and theologians advocated the practice, so that the question was finally settled in favour of the Indians by the humanity of Isabella. As the venerable bishop Las Casas observes, where the most learned men have doubted, it is not surprising that an unlettered mariner should err. These remarks in palliation of the conduct of Columbus are required by candour. It is proper to show him in connexion with the age in which he lived, lest the errors of the time should be considered his individual abuses. It is not the intention of the author, however, to justify Columbus on a point where it is inexcusable to err. Let it remain a blot on his illustrious name, and let others draw lessons from it (*A History of the Life and Voyages of Christopher Columbus* by Washington Irving, Vol. 3, Book VIII, Ch. V, pp. 199-200).

Wise words from someone who was more intelligent and eloquent than all of Columbus' critics and revisionists combined. I don't know anyone who by believing Columbus was a hero, would skip the slavery part. Yet, Columbus was a hero, in spite of slavery. Maybe what revisionists don't like is that Irving provided historical context.

Where I slightly disagree with Irving is, when he said Columbus "sinned." Imprisoning enemy combatants is not a sin. Abusing them is. Even in Bible times certain forms of slavery were allowed. God forbid the Israelites to enslave each other, unless it was temporary, due to debt. Yet, God allowed them to buy slaves from other countries or from foreigners living among them permanently. Does that make God a sinner? See Deuteronomy 24:7 and Leviticus 25:42-46.

Irving also believed that Columbus' claims that God spoke to him on several occasions, were just Columbus' imagination. That alone should be the reason for revisionists to celebrate Irving's work since some of them don't like religion that much.

Fourth, Queen Isabel indeed "offered to pawn her jewels to finance his enterprise." [2] I don't understand why Keen would call that a "legend," when it was mentioned by Ferdinand Columbus, which book Keen himself translated. Las Casas repeated the same story as well. See *The Life of the Admiral Christopher Columbus* by his son Ferdinand, Ch. 15, p. 44; and *Historia de las Indias* by Las Casas, Tomo I, Lib. I, Cap. XXXII, p. 248.

Now, let's talk about "the anecdote of the egg." The story goes like this:

> A shallow courtier present, impatient of the honours paid to Columbus, and meanly jealous of him as a foreigner, abruptly asked him whether he thought that, in case he had not discovered the Indies, there were not other men who would have been capable of the enterprise. To this, Columbus made no immediate reply, but, taking an egg, invited the company to make it stand upon one end. Every one attempted it, but in vain, where-upon he struck it upon the table so as to break the end, and left it standing on the broken part; illustrating, in this simple manner, that when he had once shown the way to the New World, nothing was easier than to follow it. [3]

The anecdote of the egg is portrayed in *Christopher Columbus: The Discovery* movie in 1992.

Though Irving was inclined to believe this story, he acknowledged that it was "condemned as trivial" by some people. The reason why he added it in his book was because it came from an Italian historian named Girolamo Benzoni, [4] and because "the universal popularity of the anecdote is a proof" in Irving's view, "of its merit." Nevertheless, Benzoni was not the best historian of his day. His 16th-century work, *History of the New World,* does have a number of factual errors. Something Benzoni got right though, was that Columbus was a hero. He called him "the invincible Christopher Columbus." [5]

I also need to add that Irving gave Columbus 20 years more of age than he was. That error came from one of Columbus' primary historical sources, Andrés Bernáldez, "commonly known as the Curate of Los Palacios" and not from Irving's imagination. [6]

As for "Columbus's opponents believed the world was flat," that's partially true. However, Irving never claimed that was the reason the Spanish council refused Columbus' proposal, or that every member of the council believed such a thing, as some Irving opponents want us to believe today. Actually, Irving accurately named the **reasons** why Columbus was rejected by the council. When Irving added the "Flat Earth" as ONE of the arguments from the council, he **probably** got the idea from primary historical source, Las Casas, when he said, "others would argue that **the world was infinite** and that would be impossible to reach the eastern limits even after years of sailing" (*History of the Indies*, Book One, Ch. 29, pp. 27-28).

Another argument of the Spanish council against Columbus was that according to St. Augustine there were no "antipodes." That is, the people who inhabited the other side of the World (*History of the Indies* by Las Casas, Book One, Ch. 29, p. 28).

According to 16th-century Spanish Jesuit missionary and naturalist José de Acosta, some people interpreted, or really misinterpreted, that St. Augustine believed that the Earth was flat. [7]

That's where it **seems** Irving got the Flat Earth as part of the story. That was not the problem, though. The problem with Irving is that he added what seems to be a fictional debate about the shape of the Earth, apparently inspired by José de Acosta's *Natural & Moral History of the Indies* book, and he used it as an artistic license to illustrate what some people might still have believed about the shape of the Earth in the 15th and 16th century. [8]

The question is: Is the Irving biography of Columbus fictional or historical? The answer is: historical. Yet, there is a handful of artistic license in it, with the fictional Flat Earth debate being the one that everyone knows and likes to quote. Yet, his work is better, and 99% more accurate than most Columbus biographies out there.

Another question I would ask is, how can a handful of artistic license in Irving's work be the equivalent to "hero myth-making"?

You may wonder, why did I even have to bring this to attention? The reason is to illustrate to the reader the hypocrisy of Columbus' revisionists. They are making a big deal of Washington Irving's work on Columbus, for a handful of artistic license that doesn't distort the Columbus story, or his heroic status, while they, themselves, have created a myth out of Columbus, as him being "Hitler," "Himmler," "evil," "a genocidal maniac," "racist," "hater," "pirate," "rapist," leader of a "child sex slavery ring," "sketchy," "opportunistic," "dishonest," "criminal," guilty of things that happened, that he had nothing to do with, or accused of conflicts in places in America that he never reached. These are the same people who grumbled against Washington Irving for taking a little artistic license, while they, themselves, have created false biographies of Columbus and myths of him, based on lies, guided by their own preconceived prejudice and hate.

Chapter 33. Samuel Eliot Morison

Samuel Eliot Morison was a 20th-century American influential historian who wrote several works on Columbus. He admired him as a sailor since Morison himself was one and he believed Columbus was a hero as well. As a historian, Morison liked to be present at the real locations when writing. During World War II he offered himself as a U.S. Navy chronicler to President Roosevelt, but he wanted to be present, living with the Navy crew during the war so he could also be a witness of the events. Likewise, Morison took an expedition with a sailing ship to recreate Columbus' voyages by following Columbus' journal and letters, while writing his famous work, *Admiral of the Ocean Sea.* [1]

However, Morison made a few false claims that are repeated today by some pro-Columbus authors as if it were historical facts. For a while, I used to wonder where those authors were getting that information from, until I noticed they named Morison as their source in their books' references and footnotes.

One of those falsehoods is that Columbus enslaved the Taínos because there was no gold. To be clear, this charge doesn't come from Morison himself, but from the authors who have used Morison's translation of Michele de Cuneo's letter as their source. In the letter, Cuneo claimed Columbus took some natives and sold them as slaves, after exploring the Caribbean during his second voyage. Since Cuneo did not explain why Columbus did so, these authors assumed it was because "there was no gold," and now those assumptions are repeated as "history." [2]

In *Admiral of the Ocean Sea,* what Morison actually claimed was that Columbus proposed the <u>enslavement of the Caribs</u> in order to pay for supplies until "the expected gold mine came to production." But then Morison complained saying that after Columbus "had declared time and again that the Taínos were the kindest, most peaceful and generous people in the world" he would end up enslaving them. [3] That statement is a gross generalization. Saying that Columbus "enslaved the Taínos" gives the impression to the reader that Columbus enslaved every native tribe he saw everywhere he went. People need to be careful with generalizations.

I wonder what Morison wanted Columbus to do after Caonabó killed his men? Make a peace treaty? Well, he did, on his first voyage with Guacanagarí. What else should Columbus have done? Go to some other place? Well, he did. Remember, he went to another place on the island, as we saw in Chapter 17. What else should Columbus have done when Caonabó tried to ambush the Spaniards at Santo Tomás fort? Nothing? Give them presents? Treat them with kindness?

If you wonder why Morison said such things, I would assume it was political correctness or just the fact he removed Columbus from historical context.

Morison also believed that Columbus' "fine servants" comment was code for slavery. He blamed Columbus for genocide as well, saying, "the policy and acts of Columbus for which he alone was responsible began the depopulation of the terrestrial paradise that was Hispaniola in 1492. Of the original natives... one third were killed off between 1494 and 1496." [4]

At this point I'm not going to repeat myself since we already explained and debunked all these allegations in previous chapters. Revisionists gladly repeat Morison's statement as gospel, because they know Morison contradictorily believed Columbus was a hero.

Question: How can one be a hero and a genocidal maniac at the same time? Besides, Columbus' policy was not one of genocide and the natives were killing one another long before 1492. Morison was wrong in this respect and many of those comments were rooted in Bartolomé de las Casas' opinions and views. Morison bought into many of Las Casas' false claims.

Morison also mistakenly claimed that thousands of natives committed suicide during this timeline of Columbus' second voyage [5]. Yet, he did not provide sources to support that claim. In fact, ALL primary sources confirmed that the mass suicides happened later after Columbus was out of office, during the abuses of the Spaniards under the Nicolás de Ovando administration.

Morison also mistranslated the Juana de las Torres letter, the part that revisionists claim Columbus incriminated himself in pedophilia or a sex slave trade. Here is his mistranslation:

Moreover, a hundred castellanos, or a farm, are paid for a woman, and this has become a common practice; there are many merchants who go looking for wenches-those of nine or ten years old are now at a premium, but a good price can be obtained for women all ages. [6]

Now, here is the original quote:

Por una muger tambien se fallan cien castellanos como por una labranza, y es mucho en uso, y ha ya fartos mercaderes que andan buscando muchachas: de nueve a diez son agora en precio: de todas edades ha de tener un bueno. [7]

Columbus did not use the word "wenches," even though that is an old word for "young girls" as well. Like revisionists, Morison confused the number of young women with their ages. Note, that Morison never said this quote was one of incrimination. Morison knew Columbus was being critical of the Spaniards' corruption in the letter, and that his tone was one of sarcasm, frustration, and anger. Interestingly, revisionists do not use Morison's translation, instead they use the correct one.

Morison claimed that during the fourth voyage, Columbus "exorcised" a waterspout that was ready to hit his ships by reading the Bible where Jesus calmed the tempest by saying, "Fear not, is I!" Then, according to Morison, Columbus with one hand with the Bible and the other with a sword "traced a cross in the sky and a circle around his whole fleet" with the sword. [8] However, according to primary source, Ferdinand Columbus, who witnessed this event, said that the waterspout was dissolved by the sailors reading the Gospel according to St. John (*The Life of the Admiral Christopher Columbus* by his son Ferdinand, Ch. 94, p. 246).

Morison did not provide a source for his claim. The story could be just a joke or a legend, but Morison never specified.

Morison would defend Columbus against the revisionists of his times. He would criticize them for seeing things that were not there. Yet for some reason, Morison did, to some extent, the same. That doesn't mean Morrison's work is bad. I personally admire his work, research, and insights, and I have used them for this book. The very few negative comments Morison made comes just from one chapter anyway (*Chapter XXXV Hell in Hispaniola*).

As much as I respect, love and enjoy Morison's works, he is not a primary source, and his opinions and interpretations were just that. The same way lawmakers are not above the law, so are historians, including the good ones. They are not above history.

Chapter 34. Columbus The Hero

Columbus was nothing revisionists claim him to be, neither today nor in the past. He was not ignorant, a pirate, a racist, dishonest, paranoid, narcissistic, ruthless, vindictive, evil or a genocidal rapist. The real Columbus was a man of faith, educated, intelligent, honest, and all the good things his contemporary and sometimes critic, Bartolomé de las Casas, told us about in Chapter 30. In other words, Columbus was exactly what revisionists claim he was not, including a **HERO**:

1. Starting with some of the most obscure Columbus stories, assuming the accounts are true, as a young man, Columbus the Hero fought enemy countries with Colombo the Younger, defended himself from pirates and corsairs, and he was also sent by King René to Tunis to capture the galleass *Fernandina* in 1472 [1] *The Life of the Admiral Christopher Columbus* by his son Ferdinand, Ch. 4, p. 11.

2. As Columbus the Hero was waiting to get approval for his enterprise in 1489, "Diego Ortiz de Zuñiga, in his Annals of Seville, says that the Sovereigns wrote to that city directing lodgings and accommodations to be furnished to Christopher Columbus, who was coming there to the court for a conference of importance. The city fulfilled the command, but the conference was postponed and interrupted by the campaign 'in which,' adds the author, 'the

same Columbus was found fighting, giving proofs of the distinguished valour which accompanied his wisdom, and his lofty desires.' " [2]

3.	Columbus the Hero did what no one would dare to do in his times: Travel from Europe to the Indies, which the "professionals" told him he could not do, while the sailors threatened to throw him overboard if he would not return home. He chose to complete his voyage, and the rest is history.

4.	During his first voyage, Columbus the Hero gave gifts to the natives, traded with them, and would not let the Spaniards exploit them in their dealings. He said: "I have given the men orders everywhere to take care not to do the least thing to displease them and not to take anything from them against their will, so they have paid them for everything." He ended that voyage on peaceful terms with them, and promised Chief Guacanagarí, that he would get rid of the Caribs (cannibals) for him. *Columbus' Journal translated* by John Cummins, Friday, December 21, 1492.

5.	As Columbus the Hero was about to end his first voyage, he stood by his men, when Portuguese authorities seized them, right after a storm blew their ships away to Portuguese territory. *The Life of the Admiral Christopher Columbus* by his son Ferdinand, Chapters 38-41.

6.	Columbus the Hero begins his second voyage by rescuing natives from the hands of the cannibals. When Columbus returned to Hispaniola, he found the 39 men he left there, during his first voyage, dead. The Spaniards told him to arrest his ally Chief Guacanagarí, but Columbus the Hero chose not to, until it was confirmed it was Caonabó, and not Guacanagarí, the person responsible for the murders.

7. Columbus the Hero fought with his ally Guacanagarí at his side, against Caonabó and the other chiefs, for killing one of Guacanagarí's wives and kidnapping another. In that way, Columbus brought Caonabó to justice for also killing his 39 Spaniards and to stop him from his constant attempts to assassinate him.

8. During this second voyage, Columbus the Hero went sailing again, with the purpose of exploration, but also with the intention of getting rid of the cannibals.

9. While Columbus the Hero was on his way back to Spain (to end his second voyage), some Spaniards suggested eating the natives, as they ran out of provisions, signaling that they might starve to death. Columbus the Hero forbade them to commit such an act of inhumanity.

10. Columbus the Hero went to rescue two Spanish vessels from French corsairs as he was departing to sail for his third voyage. *The Life of the Admiral Christopher Columbus* by his son Ferdinand, Ch. 66, pp. 175-176.

11. Outnumbered, Columbus the Hero unsuccessfully fought against Roldan's rebellion, but he sent letters to Spain asking for help and he complained how the Spaniards were mistreating the natives.

12. Columbus the Hero initiated his fourth voyage by rescuing a Portuguese ship that was under attack by the Moors (Muslims). Though the "Moors had already raised the

siege," the Portuguese Captain "gave profuse thanks to the Admiral for the courtesy and for the offer of help." *The Life of the Admiral Christopher Columbus* by his son Ferdinand, Ch. 88, p. 227.

13.   Columbus the Hero defeated the Porras brothers' mutiny during his last and fourth voyage.

14.   Columbus the Hero was also looking to help pay for a crusade to save Christ's empty tomb at the Holy Land from Muslim invaders. *Historia de las Indias* by Las Casas, Tomo I, Lib. I, Cap. II, p. 45.

It doesn't matter where Columbus was, he was always fighting. Fighting myths, ridicule, mockery, condescending people, or fighting corsairs, pirates, mutineers, cannibals, criminals, rebels, sometimes even nature, like hurricanes, storms, waterspouts, shipwrecks, and even being marooned on an island like Robinson Crusoe. And that's just a taste of his struggles. In fact, I purposely haven't told many of the stories of Columbus, because I want you, the reader, to read the stories for yourself. I promise it will be one of the most amazing historical accounts you will ever read. Also, you will be able to compare notes with Columbus' biography vs. the revisionist versions and claims and see for yourself that revisionists are not telling you the truth about Columbus. If you want the full story of Columbus from a primary historical source, I would suggest starting with *The Life of the Admiral Christopher Columbus* by his son Ferdinand. Just be aware of a few unflattering comments and innuendos about Columbus made by the translator, Benjamin Keen, in his *Introduction*.

After all the grumbling from his critics, Columbus ended up fulfilling his promises: No " 'single person was more responsible for Spain's expanded dominions than Columbus. He planted the Christian faith in places so foreign and far,' Oviedo wrote, and because of him, 'so many treasures of gold, and silver, and pearls and other riches and trade goods went to Spain. No other Spaniard ever brought such wealth to the kingdom.' " [3]

As a hero, the most important thing Columbus exported to the New World was the gospel of Christ; Christ being the most important of all heroes, because He died in our place to save us from our sins and rose from the dead to set us free. Now, I understand that if you are not *religious*, that statement won't be appealing to you. However, Columbus also exported the ideas of Western civilization, and it was men of faith and Western ideas who later brought us freedom of worship, freedom of expression, freedom from slavery, individual rights, civil rights, human rights, the advancement of science and medicine, curing or treating some of the sicknesses revisionists complain about, including syphilis and smallpox, thus blessing men of all races and all walks of life. So why are revisionists complaining again? If it wasn't for these exported values, uncivilized natives would still be practicing cannibalism, human sacrifices, and slavery today.

If revisionists know anything about history, they should know that Christopher Columbus is the most important person in history, after Jesus Christ. The same way Christ divided history, before Christ and after Christ, so it is with Columbus, who divided history as the pre-Columbian era, and the Columbus era. I guess if one can hate Jesus Christ, then it is no wonder they can distort the story of the one who expanded the Christian religion to the New World.

Columbus also united two worlds: The Old and the New. Two worlds that for some reason lost contact with one another for centuries. He united these two worlds for better, and not for worse. As for those Spaniards who abused the natives in the past, no one should worry. Divine justice is real, and I'm sure they are in a special place in Hell for the massacres that they committed.

We have people with agendas spreading misinformation today. Ironically, they always begin their grief against American history with Columbus, after they deny that Columbus discovered America, or had anything or little to do with American history. They use propaganda to try to indoctrinate us against God, Christianity, Judeo-Christian values, Western values, Objective Truth, Moral Absolutes, Natural Law, etc. And then we wonder why so many kids are burning college buildings, American flags, hating their own country, and participating in subversive activities, including domestic terrorism. In other words, they are acting like the Spanish Conquistadores they claim they hate.

These anti-Columbus activists, professors, writers, and the like, constantly use fictitious historical events to make political and philosophical talking points, thus making false conclusions that are based on false narratives. If Columbus was alive today, he could sue them for defamation and slander, and he would win.

They are upset with Columbus and the Europeans for establishing themselves in other countries and imposing their culture on the natives, while they impose their views on our children. They lament the genocide that happened five hundred years ago, while many of them sympathize with communism, which is responsible for the genocide of millions of people in Asia and Europe in recent history.

Revisionists are also making the whole Columbus story a racial issue, when it has nothing to do with race. But then they judge people by the color of their skin, and not by the content of their character. In other words, Columbus and the Europeans were "bad" people, because they were white, and the colored peoples are permanent victims of a white majority, or white privilege, just because they are "dark." They love to shame people for being white, even though many revisionists are white. Enter

the race industry. Enter the grief industry. They demand "repa-rations" for slavery we don't practice anymore, thus forgetting that slavery was practiced throughout history by people of all skin colors, including natives and blacks. They claim to be anti-racists, while they make racist statements against the Europeans who colonized America. In that way, revisionists keep us divided and bitter over events that happened long ago, that we,
today, have nothing to do with. "Divide and conquer." That's their motto.

If Columbus' legacy is one of misery and destruction, why then do we have more prosperity and freedom in the New World than the Old?

Let's assume that some, or perhaps, all these allegations against Columbus are true:

Columbus was arrested, humiliated, begged God for forgiveness, was discredited, died forgotten, unappreciated, and at the end of it all, the continent was named after someone else. What else do revisionists want him to do to pay for his alleged wrongs? Where are the second chances? Where is the tolerance and understanding some Americans claim to have?

On the other hand, every American country should honor Christopher Columbus one way or another. Today we are in America because of Columbus, as a consequence of his dis-coveries and settlement. In the United States, we should keep celebrating Columbus Day, because without Columbus, there wouldn't have been Pilgrims; without the Pilgrims we wouldn't have Thanksgiving and Thanksgiving Day; Independence and Independence Day; Presidents and Presidents Day; veterans and Veterans Day; Martin Luther King, Jr. and the rest of our federal holidays.

Even the "Pledge of Allegiance" was written to comme-morate the four hundredth anniversary of Columbus' discovery of America. [4] Francis Bellamy was a Christian minister, but interestingly, he was a socialist who unlike some modern socialists, he admired Columbus. His "Pledge of Allegiance" was first published on September 8, 1892, in a popular children's magazine named *The Youth's Companion* with the purpose of instilling patriotism in students. [5]

Today they want to instill in students a hatred for America. Why should we expect people to love America and what it stands for, if its history is being distorted, starting with the biography of the one who discovered it!? No wonder some people won't recite the "Pledge of Allegiance," or stand during the American Anthem. We need to stop the insanity, otherwise, Thanksgiving Day is next.

My hope is that this work will somehow spread the truth about Columbus and his legacy. I hope that parents teach this truth to their children. I hope teachers teach the truth to their students. I hope the media retract their false biographies and accusations on Columbus and correct their mistakes. I hope people will stop sharing false information in social media, without first double-checking the facts.

I would like to close this book with some final words from Washington Irving, from his biography of Columbus. This is what he said:

> His conduct as a discoverer was characterized by the grandeur of his views, and the magnanimity of his spirit. Instead of scouring the newly found countries, like a grasping adventurer eager only for immediate gain, as was too generally the case with contemporary discoverers, he sought to ascertain their soil and productions, their rivers and harbours. He was desirous of colonizing and cultivating them, of conciliating and civilizing the natives, of building cities, introducing the useful arts, sub-

jecting everything to the control of law, order and religion, and thus of founding regular and prosperous empires. In this glorious plan, he was constantly defeated by the dissolute rabble which he was doomed to command; with whom all law was tyranny, and order restraint. They interrupted all useful works by their seditions, provoked the peaceful Indians to hostility, and after they had thus pulled misery and warfare upon their own heads, and overwhelmed Columbus with the ruins of the edifice he was building, they charged him with being the cause of the confusion. Well would it have been for Spain, had her discoverers who followed in the track of Columbus possessed his sound policy and liberal views. What dark pages would have been spared in her colonial history! The new world, in such case, would have been settled by peaceful colonists, and civilized by enlightened legislators, instead of being overrun by desperate adventurers, and desolated by avaricious conquerors...

In his letters and journals, instead of detailing circumstances with the technical precision of a mere voyager, he notices the beauties of nature with the enthusiasm of a poet or a painter...

When surrounded and overwhelmed by the ingratitude and violence of worthless men, he often, in the retirement of his cabin, gave way to gushes of sorrow, and relieved his overladen heart by sighs and groans. When he returned in chains to Spain, and came in the presence of Isabella, instead of continuing the lofty pride with which he had hitherto sustained his injuries, he was touched with grief and tenderness at her sympathy, and burst forth into sobs and tears.

He was devoutly pious: religion mingled with the whole course of his thoughts and actions, and shines forth in all his most private and unstudied writings. Whenever he made any great discovery, he celebrated it by solemn thanks to God. The voice of prayer, and the melody of praise, rose from his ships when they first beheld the new world, and his first action on landing, was to prostrate himself upon the earth and render up thanksgivings...

To his intellectual vision it was given to read in the signs of the times, and in the conjectures and reveries of past ages, the indications of an unknown world; as soothsayers were said to read predictions in the stars, and to foretel events from the visions of the night. 'His soul,' observes a Spanish writer, 'was superior to the age in which he lived. For him was reserved the great enterprize to plough a sea which had given rise to so many fables, and to decipher the mystery of his time.' *A History of the Life and Voyages of Christopher Columbus* by Washington Irving, Vol. 3, Book VIII, Ch. V, pp. 196-199, and p. 201.

"God is just and he will see that the truth is known."
 -Christopher Columbus

The End

Endnotes

Chapter 1. Hearsay

1. Snopes: " 'Indigenous Peoples' Day' Movement Continues to Grow. The push comes as Columbus Day receives increasing criticism for erasing the historical contributions of indigenous people of the Americas" by Brooke Binkowski, October 2016.
https://www.snopes.com/news/2016/10/10/indigenous-peoples-day-movement-continues-to-grow/

The New York Times: Sunday Book Review, "The Less Than Heroic Christopher Columbus" by Ian W. Toll, Sept. 23, 2011.
http://www.nytimes.com/2011/09/25/books/review/columbus-the-four-voyages-by-laurence-bergreen-book-review.html

Bio. Channel: "Christopher Columbus: Hero or Villain? Columbus Day churns up a stormy sea of controversy every year" by. B. Myint, Oct. 12, 2015.
https://www.biography.com/news/christopher-columbus-day-facts

MTV News: "Columbus Was a Genocidal Rapist | Decoded | MTV News" Published on
https://www.youtube.com/watch?v=UbG7VbebC_Y

The Huffington Post: "Columbus Day? True Legacy: Cruelty and Slavery" by Eric Kasum. 10/11/2010 01:46 am ET | Updated Oct 10, 2016.
http://www.huffingtonpost.com/eric-kasum/columbus-day-a-bad-idea_b_742708.html

DailyKos: "Columbus and The Legacy of Genocide" by Nican Tlaca, Saturday, Oct. 12, 2013.
http://www.dailykos.com/story/2013/10/11/1246553/-Columbus-and-The-Legacy-of-Genocide

2. Pew Research: "Working on Columbus Day? It depends on where you live" by Drew Desilver, October 8, 2015. Originally published Oct. 14, 2013.
http://www.pewresearch.org/fact-tank/2015/10/08/working-on-columbus-day-it-depends-on-where-you-live/

3. Smithsonian: "The Timeline History of Celebrating (and Not Celebrating) Columbus Day. The holiday has been controversial practically since its inception" by Rebeca Coleman, October 10, 2016.
http://www.smithsonianmag.com/history/timeline-history-celebrating-and-not-celebrating-columbus-day-180960736/#cFkUcxcaPUyyhF9s.99

4. Natives News Online: "Hundreds of American Indians to Gather on Alcatraz Island for (Un) Thanksgiving Day Sunrise Ceremony" by Levi Rickert, 27 Nov. 2013.

UAINE: "Boston.com 2014 article: National Day of Mourning Reflects on Thanksgiving's Horrific, Bloody History. Thanksgiving: A National Day of Mourning for Indians," 1998 by Moonanum James and Mahtowin Munro. http://www.uaine.org/

Chapter 2. The Historical Sources vs. The Revisionists

1. "Columbus parade could see less strife. Churchill, conflict having an effect" by Charlie Brennan, Rocky Mountain News September 24, 2005.
http://www.transformcolumbusday.org/media/20050924-rm.htm

2. "History Not Taught is History Forgot: Columbus' Legacy of Genocide." Excerpted from the book "Indians are Us" by Ward Churchill. Common Courage Press, 1994.
http://www.mit.edu/~thistle/v9/9.11/1columbus.html

Chapter 3. Discover, not "Discover"

1. Encyclopedia Britannica: Christopher Columbus Italian Explorer. Written by: Valerie I.J. Flint. Last Updated 1-14-2016.
https://www.britannica.com/biography/Christopher-Columbus

2. Encyclopedia Britannica: Amerigo Vespucci, Italian Navigator, Written by: Roberto Almagià. Last Updated: 10-17-2011. https://www.britannica.com/biography/Amerigo-Vespucci

3. MTV News: "Columbus Was a Genocidal Rapist | Decoded |MTV News" Published on Oct 9, 2015. https://www.youtube.com/watch?v=UbG7VbebC_Y

4. The Voyage of Christopher Columbus by John Cummins, Introduction, "The Orient and the Ocean Sea," p. 9.

5. The Saga of Eirik the Red, Chapter "Eirik's Family, and his son Leif's Discovery of Vinland," pp. 23-27.

6. The Enemies of Christopher Columbus by Bowden, p. 27.

7. Ibid, p. 28.

Chapter 4. The Christ Bearer

1. The New York Times: Sunday Book Review, "The Less Than Heroic Christopher Columbus" by Ian W. Toll, Sept. 23, 2011.
http://www.nytimes.com/2011/09/25/books/review/columbus-the-four-voyages-by-laurence-bergreen-book-review.html

2. *Bartholomew de las Casas* by MacNutt, Chapter II, p. 14.

3. *Admiral of the Ocean Sea* by Morison, Chapter XXXVII, "Preparations" p. 505.

Chapter 5. Pirate of the Caribbean

1. *The Life of the Admiral Christopher Columbus by his son Ferdinand,* Introduction, xxxviii.

2. Ibid, Chapter 5, pp. 12-14.

3. *A History of the Life and Voyages of Christopher Columbus* by Washington Irving, Vol. 3, Appendix No. VIII, p. 254.

4. *The Life of the Admiral Christopher Columbus by his son Ferdinand*, Notes to Chapter 1-5, Note # 2 from Chapter 5, pp. 288-289.

Chapter 6. The Flat Earth

1. "Christopher Columbus: Hero or Villain?" "Columbus Day churns up a stormy sea of controversy every year," by B. Myint, Oct. 12, 2015.
http://www.biography.com/news/christopher-columbus-day-facts

2. *A People's History of the United States* by Zinn, Chapter 1. "Columbus, The Indians, and Human Progress," pp. 1-2.

3. *Isabella: The Warrior Queen* by Kirstin Downey, Chapter Fifteen. "Landing in Paradise," p. 236.

Chapter 7. Mutiny

1. *Lies my Teacher Told Me* by Loewen, Chapter 2, p. 49. The New Press, New York. 1995.

2. Las Casas' archaic Spanish update is mine. Here is the original quote: "... y hablan comenzado á murmurar del viaje y de quien en él los habia puesto... comenzáronlas á manifestar, y desvergonzadamente decirle en la cara que los habia engañado y los llevaba perdidos á matar, y que juraban á tal y á cual, que sino se tornaba que lo habían primero á él de echar en la mar... con muy dulces y amorosas palabras... los esforzaba, y animaba, y rogaba... Con estas y otras palabras cumplía lo que de su parte podía..." *Historia de las Indias* by Las Casas, Tomo I, Libro I, Capítulo XXXVI, p. 268 and Capítulo XXXVII, p. 274.

3. Herrera's archaic Spanish update is mine. Here is the original quote: "... tanto mas fe acrecentaba el miedo de la Gente, i tomaban ocafion de murmurar... que para quitar contiendas, era lo mejor echarle á la Mar con difimulacion, i decir, que desgraciadamente havia caído, mientras eltaba embebido en confiderar las Eftrellas... Chriftoval... á veces con buenas palabras, i otras advirtiendo de el caftigo que fe les daria, fi le impidiefen el Viage..." *Historia General* by Herrera, Década I, Libro I, Capítulo X, p. 17.

4. *Lies my Teacher Told Me* by Loewen, Chapter 2, p. 49.

5. *The Life of the Admiral Christopher Columbus by his son Ferdinand,* Chapter 11, pp. 35-36.

Chapter 8. First to See Land

1. Las Casas' archaic Spanish update is mine. Here is the original quote: "Vido la tierra primero un marinero que se llamaba Rodrigo de Triana, pero los 10.000 maravedís de juro, sentenciaron los Reyes que los llevase Cristóbal Colón, juzgando, que, pues él habia visto primero la lumbre, fué visto ver primero la tierra.De donde podemos colegir un no chico argumento de la bondad y justicia de Dios, el cual aun en este mundo remunera como también castiga, respondiendo á la confianza que de su providencia se tiene, y á los trabajos y solicitud virtuosa de cada uno, en que ordenó, que, ansí como habia Cristóbal Colon llevado lo más trabajoso y angustioso de todo el viaje, con padecer sobre sí la parte que dello le cabia como á particular persona, y la carga de todos como pública, con los desacatos y turbaciones y aflicciones que muchas veces todos le causaron, y solo él tuvo fe firme y perseverante constancia de la divinal providencia, que no habia de ser de su fin defraudado, él alcanzase este favor, y se le atribuyese haber primero visto la tierra por ver primero la lumbre en ella, en figura de la espiritual, que, por sus sudores y trabajos, habia Cristo de infundir en aquestas gentes que vivían en tan profundas tinieblas, y ansí gozase de la merced de los 10.000 maravedís; lo cual es de estimar, no tanto por el valor dellos, como fuese tan poco, cuanto por el alegría y consuelo que en esto, aun tan minimo temporal, favoreciéndole, quiso concederle." *Historia de las Indias* by Las Casas, Tomo I, Libro I, Capítulo XXXIX, p. 289.

Chapter 9. Thanking God First

1. *Lies my Teacher Told Me,* Chapter 2, p. 50.

2. Ibid, p. 53.

3. Las Casas' archaic Spanish update is mine. Here is the original quote: "Sacó el Almirante la bandera real, y los dos Capitanes sendas banderas de la cruz verde, que el Almirante Rebaba en todos los navios por seña y divisa, con una F, que significa el rey D.Fernando, y una I, por la reina Doña Isabel, y encima de cada letra su corona... Saltando en tierra el Almirante y todos, hincan las rodillas, dan gracias inmensas al todopoderoso Dios y Señor, muchos derramando lágrimas, que los había traído á salvamento... Luego el Almirante... tomó, posesión de la dicha isla..." *Historia de las Indias* by Las Casas, Tomo I, Libro I, Capítulo XL, p. 292.

4. Herrera's archaic Spanish update is mine. Here is the original quote: "... el Almirante, con la Barca armada, i el Eitandarte Real tendido, falio á Tierra, i lo mifmo hicieron los Capitanes Martin Alonfo Pinçon, i Vicente Yañez Pinçon, con las Vanderas de la Emprefa, que era vna Cruz verde, con ciertas Coronas, i los Nombres de los Reies Católicos i haviendo todos befado la Tierra, i arrodillados, dado gracias á Dios, con lagrimas, por la gracia que les havia hecho, el Almirante fe levantó, i llamó San Salvador aquella Isla... i con la folemnidad, i palabras necefarias, tomó la pofefion en nombre de los Reies Católicos..." *Historia General* by Herrera, Década I, Libro I, Capítulo XII, p. 20.

Chapter 10. The Arrival

1. *Writings of Christopher Columbus,* p. 46.

2. Ibid, p. 62.

3. *The First Four Voyages of Amerigo Vespucci,* p. 17.

4. "Also, in the other places the men hide their women from us because of jealousy, but not here, and some of the women are very fine-bodied, and they were the first to come and give thanks to Heaven for our arrival and to bring us whatever they had, especially foodstuffs, *aje* bread, and peanuts, and five or six kinds of fruit, which I have ordered to be preserved to bring to Your Majesties." *Columbus' Journal,* translated by John Cummins, Friday 21, December 1492.

5. Spanish navigator "Enciso anchored off the coast of Caramairiana in the harbour of Carthagena, celebrated for the chastity and grace of its women, and the courage of both sexes of the inhabitants." *De Orbe Novo* by Peter Martyr, The Second Decade, Book I, p. 197.

Chapter 11. They Would Make Fine Servants

1. *A People's History of the United States* by Zinn, Chapter 1. "Columbus, The Indians, and Human Progress," p. 1.

2. This is how the Spanish version says it: "Ellos deben ser buenos servidores." *Historia de las Indias* by Las Casas, Libro I, Capítulo XL. https://es.wikisource.org/wiki/Diario_de_a_bordo_del_primer_viaje_de_Crist%C3 %B3bal_Col%C3%B3n

Chapter 12. No King, No Religion

1. *Lies my Teacher Told Me,* p. 57.

2. *A Brief Account of the Destruction of the Indies* by Las Casas, p. 6.

Chapter 13. Racist

1. *Lies my Teacher Told Me,* p. 58.

2. Ibid, p. 43.

3. *The Life of the Admiral Christopher Columbus,* Notes to Chapters 44-52, Note 2 from Chapter 47, p. 297.

Chapter 14. Shipwrecked

1. *The Four Voyages* by Bergreen, Chapter 3. "Shipwreck," p. 85.

Chapter. 15. Cannibals

1. "Taino" means "good." *De Orbe Novo* by Peter Martyr, The First Decade, Book II, p. 81.

Chapter 16. What Revisionists Claim Happened

1. *Journals and Other Documents on the Life and Voyages of Christopher Columbus* by Morison, p. 204.

2. *Lies my Teacher Told Me*, pp. 51-52.

3. *A People's History of the United States* by Zinn, Chapter 1. "Columbus, The Indians, and Human Progress," p. 4.

Chapter 17. What Really Happened

1. *Christopher Columbus* by J. H. Langille, Chapter XI. "The New Enterprises of the Colony," p. 237.

Chapter 18. No Death or Destruction

1. Michele de Cuneo claimed the Spaniards killed 16 or 18 natives. If this is true, let me remind the reader that this was in self-defense. *Journals and Other Documents on the Life and Voyages of Christopher Columbus* by Morison, p. 222.

Chapter 19. The Cutting of Hands

1. *Journals and Other Documents on the Life and Voyages of Christopher Columbus* by Morison, p. 226.

2. *Admiral of the Ocean Sea* by Morison, Chapter XXXV. "Hell in Hispaniola," p. 487.

Chapter 20. Diseases, Starvation, and Death

1. *Journals and Other Documents on the Life and Voyages of Christopher Columbus* by Morison, p. 227.

2. *Lies my Teacher Told Me* by Loewen, Chapter 2 p. 52.

3. *Admiral of the Ocean Sea* by Morison, Chapter XXXV. "Hell in Hispaniola," p. 484.

Chapter 21. Gold and Greed

1. *A People's History of the United States* by Zinn, Chapter 1. "Columbus, The Indians, and Human Progress," p. 4.

2. *A History of the Life and Voyages of Christopher Columbus* by Washington Irving, Volume 3, Book XV, Chapter VI, page 52, Footnote.

Chapter 22. Slavery, the Unpardonable Sin

1. *Bartholomew de las Casas* by MacNutt, Preface XV.

2. *Historia de las Indias* by Las Casas, Libro I, Tomo II, Capítulo CXII, pp. 129-130.

3. "Niño brought a dispatch from the Sovereigns... and a letter from the Admiral stating that the slave trade could go on, provided the victims were genuine prisoners of war." *Admiral of the Ocean Sea* by Morison, Chapter XLI. "Terrestrial Inferno," pp. 562-563. See also *Historia de las Indias* by Las Casas, Libro I, Tomo II, Capítulo CXIII, p. 135.

4. Girolamo Benzoni wrote: "Not long after I had reached *Cubagua* there arrived Pedro de Herrera, governor of the island of *Margarita*, with two brigs, accompanied by thirty Spaniards, intending to go to Terra Firma to get some slaves... After two days we left *Cumaná*, and coasting along towards the east, by the gulf of *Paria*, we landed very frequently to give the friendly petty chiefs some Spanish wine, or a shirt, or a knife from the governor, and thus induced them to send some of their vassals, or subjects, to shew us places up the country, where we might capture some Indians who were bitter enemies to them, because they were friends and confederates of the Christians." *History of the New World*, Book I, pp. 3-5.

Chapter 24. Amerigo vs. Columbus

1. *A History of the Life and Voyages of Christopher Columbus* by Washington Irving, Vol. 3, Appendix No. IX. Amerigo Vespucci, p. 279.

2. Wikipedia: "New World" Article, 2017. https://en.wikipedia.org/wiki/New_World

3. *A Brief Account of the Destruction of the Indies* by Las Casas, p. 6.

4. *The Journal of Christopher Columbus*, "Documents Relating to the Voyages of John Cabot and Gaspar Corte Real," p. 198.

5. Ibid, p. 203.

6. *The First Four Voyages of Amerigo Vespucci*, p. 22 and 23.

Chapter 25. The Spaniards vs. Columbus

1. *Admiral of the Ocean Sea* by Morison, Chapter XLIX. "Rescue and End," p. 669.

Chapter 26. Mutilations, Cruelty, and Fake Biography

1. History Channel: Christopher Columbus
http://www.history.com/topics/exploration/christopher-columbus

2. "Lost document reveals Columbus as tyrant of the Caribbean" by Giles Tremlett. Monday 7 August 2006 04.40 EDT First published on Monday 7 August 2006. https://www.google.com/amp/s/amp.theguardian.com/world/2006/aug/07/books.spain

3. Wikipedia: "Corporal punishment" Article, 2017. https://en.wikipedia.org/wiki/Corporal_punishment

Encyclopedia Britannica: "Corporal punishment" written by, The Editors of Britannica, Last Updated:1-27-2012. https://www.britannica.com/topic/corporal-punishment

Wikipedia: "Cropping" Article, 2017. https://en.wikipedia.org/wiki/Cropping_(punishment)

4. *The Book of Ser Marco Polo,* Volume 1, Book 1, Chapter LV, p. 266.

5. *A History of the Life and Voyages of Christopher Columbus* by Washington Irving, Volume 2, Book III, Chapter IV, p. 325.

6. *Bartholomew de Las Casas* by MacNutt, Appendix I- The Brevissima Relacion, p. 276.

7. *A History of the Life and Voyages of Christopher Columbus* by Washington Irving, Volume 2, Book IX, Chapter III, p. 149.

Chapter 27. The Imaginary Child Sex Slavery Ring

1. The Huffington Post "Columbus Day? True Legacy: Cruelty and Slavery" October 10, 2016. By Eric Kasum. http://www.huffingtonpost.com/eric-kasum/columbus-day-a-bad-idea_b_742708.html

Chapter 28. Genocide

1. *Bartholomew de las Casas* by MacNutt, Preface, XIV.

2. *A History of the Life and Voyages of Christopher Columbus* by Washington Irving, Volume 3, Book VII, Chapter IV, pp. 160-161. Columbus' letter quoted by Washington Irving also appears in *Historia de las Indias* by Las Casas, Libro II, Tomo III, Capítulo XXXVII, p. 190.

Chapter 29. Constructive Criticism

1. *The Voyage of Christopher Columbus* by John Cummins, Introduction, p. 39.

2. *The First Four Voyages of Amerigo Vespucci,* p. 17. *The First Voyage Round the World* by Antonio Pigafetta p. 46. *Historia General* by Oviedo, Lib. XVII, Cap. XXVIII, p. 575.

Chapter 30. Michele de Cuneo

1. *Journals and Other Documents on the Life and Voyages of Christopher Columbus* by Morison, p. 209.

2. Ibid, p. 212.

3. Ibid, p. 210 and 214 note 1.

4. *The Life of the Admiral Christopher Columbus* by his son Ferdinand, Chapter 74, p. 192. Also, Note # 2 from Chapter 74, p. 301.

5. See https://www.dictionary.com/

6. *Journals and Other Documents on the Life and Voyages of Christopher Columbus* by Morison, pp. 211-212.

7. Ibid, Syllacio's Letter to Duke of Milan, p. 236.

8. Ibid, pp. 219-220.

Chapter 31. Bartolomé de las Casas

1. "Viggo Mortensen reads Bartolome de las Casas." Published on Jan. 27, 2008. Voices of a People's History of the United States. https://www.youtube.com/watch?v=_nxRvt5Rjx8

2. *Bartholomew de las Casas* by MacNutt, Chapter XXI.- "San Gregorio de Valladolid. Last Labours. The Death of Las Casas," p. 246.

3. *Bartholomew de las Casas* by MacNutt, Chapter XX.- "Las Casas Arrives at Valladolid. The Thirty Propositions. Debate with Gines de Sepulveda," p. 232.

4. *The Four Voyages* by Bergreen, Epilogue, p. 365.

5. *The Voyage of Christopher Columbus*, John Cummins, Introduction, p. 4.

Chapter 32. Washington Irving vs The Myth Makers

1. *The Life of the Admiral Christopher Columbus* by his son Ferdinand, translated and edited by Benjamin Keen, Introduction XXXV.

2. *A History of the Life and Voyages of Christopher Columbus* by Washington Irving, Volume 1, Book II, Chapter VII, "Application to the Court at the Time of the Surrender of Granada."

3. *A History of the Life and Voyages of Christopher Columbus* by Washington Irving, Volume 1, Book V, Chapter VII, "Sojourn of Columbus at Barcelona. Attentions paid him by the Sovereigns and Courtiers."

4. *A History of the Life and Voyages of Christopher Columbus* by Washington Irving, Volume 1, Book V, Chapter VII, "Sojourn of Columbus at Barcelona. Attentions paid him by the Sovereigns and Courtiers." Footnote 1.

5. *History of the New World* by Benzoni, Book I, p. 2.

6. *A History of the Life and Voyages of Christopher Columbus* by Washington Irving, Volume 1, Book 1, Chapter 1, "Birth, Parentage, and Education of Columbus." Footnote #1; and *Historia de los Reyes Católicos* by Andrés Bernáldez, Capítulo CXXXI, p. 334.
7. *The Natural & Moral History of the Indies* by José de Acosta, Chapter IV. "Containing an answere to that which is obiected out of the holy Scripture, against the roundnes of the earth," p. 13.

8. *A History of the Life and Voyages of Christopher Columbus* by Washington Irving, Volume 1, Book II, Chapter IV. "Columbus before the Council at Salamanca," Footnote 1 Acosta, l. i, cap. 1.

Chapter 33. Samuel Eliot Morison

1. https://www.smithsonianmag.com/history/revisiting-samuel-eliot-morisons-landmark-history-63715/

2. *Journals and Other Documents on the Life and Voyages of Christopher Columbus* by Morison, p. 226.

3. *Admiral of the Ocean Sea* by Morison, Chapter XXXV. "Hell in Hispaniola," p. 486.

4. Ibid, p. 493.

5. Ibid, p. 492.

6. *Journals and Other Documents on the Life and Voyages of Christopher Columbus* by Morison, Columbus's Letter to Doña Juana de las Torres, p. 294.

7. *Select Letters of Christopher Columbus*, p. 164.

8. *Admiral of the Ocean Sea* by Morison, Chapter XLV. Veragua, p. 619.

Chapter 34. Columbus The Hero

1. Benjamin Keen said the event took place in 1472 (*The Life of the Admiral Christopher Columbus* by his son Ferdinand, Notes to Chapters 1-5, Note #1 from Chapter 4, p. 288). James Hibbert Langille said it happened in 1473 (*Christopher Columbus* by James Hibbert Langille, Introduction, p. 23).

2. *Anales Eclesiasticos y Seculares de la Ciudad de Sevilla* by Diego Ortiz de Zuñiga, Tomo III, Libro XII, Año 1489, p. 145. Part of the quote of the English translation of Zuñiga's account came from *A History of the Life and Voyages of Christopher Columbus* by Washington Irving, Volume 1, Book II, Chapter V, "Further Applications at the Court of Castile. Columbus Follows the Court in its Campaigns."

3. I don't agree with Downey's view on Columbus, but she is right with this, especially since she was quoting primary historical sources. *Isabella: The Warrior Queen* by Kirstin Downey, Chapter Seventeen "Lands of Vanity and Illusion," p. 297. See *Historia General* by Oviedo, Lib. III, Cap. IX, p. 81.

4. *The Enemies of Christopher Columbus* by Bowden, p. 71.

5. Bellamy, Francis, "The Story of the Pledge of Allegiance to the Flag," University of Rochester Volume VIII · Winter 1953· Number 2, The Story of The Pledge of Allegiance to The Flag -Francis Bellamy, '76. http://rbscp.lib.rochester.edu/3418

Bibliography

The Voyage of Christopher Columbus, Columbus' Own Journal of Discovery. Newly Restored and Translated by John Cummins. St. Martin's Press New York, 1992.

The Journal of Christopher Columbus (During his First Voyage 1492-1493) and Documents Relating to the Voyages of John Cabot and Gaspar Corte Real, Works Issued by The Hakluyt Society, London. No. LXXXVI.

Writings of Christopher Columbus, Descriptive of the Discovery and Occupation of the New World. Charles L. Webster & Co. New York, 1890.

Select Letters of Christopher Columbus, With Other Original Documents Related to His Four Voyages to the New World. Second Edition. Works Issued by The Hakluyt Society, London. M, DCCC.LXX.

Relaciones y Cartas de Cristóbal Colón. Imprenta de la Viuda de Hernando y C. ª Ferraz, 13. Madrid. 1892.

The Book of Prophecies Edited by Christopher Columbus. Wipf & Stock Publishers, Eugene, Oregon, 1997.

The Life of the Admiral Christopher Columbus by his son Ferdinand. Translated and Annotated by Benjamin Keen. Rutgers University Press. New Brunswick, New Jersey 1992.

De Orbe Novo. The Eight Decades of Peter Martyr D'Anghera. G. P. Putnam's Sons, New York and London The Kníckerbocker Press, 1912.

History of the Indies by Bartolome de las Casas. Translated and Edited by Andree M. Collard. Harper Torchbooks Harper & Row, Publishers, New York, Evanston, and London, 1971.

Historia de las Indias, Escrita por Fray Bartolomé de las Casas, Obispo de Chiapa, Imprenta de Miguel Ginesta, 1875.

A Brief Account of the Destruction of the Indies by Bartolome de las Casas, The Project Gutenberg EBook, 2007.

Historia General de los Hechos de los Castellanos, en las Islas, y Tierra-Firme de el Mar Oceano. Escrita por Antonio de Herrera.

Historia de los Reyes Católicos, Crónica inédita del siglo XV, por El Bachiller Andrés Bernáldez. Tomo I. Imprenta y librería de D. José Alaria Zamora, 1856.

Historia General y Natural de las Indias, Isla y Tierra-Firme del Mar Océano por El Capitán Gonzalo Fernández de Oviedo y Valdés. Primer Cronista del Nuevo Mundo. Imprenta de la Real Academia de la Historia, Madrid, 1851.

A History of the Life and Voyages of Christopher Columbus in Four Volumes by Washington Irving. Published by A. and W. Galignani, 1828.

Admiral of the Ocean Sea. A Life of Christopher Columbus by Samuel Eliot Morison. Little Brown and Company, Boston, Toronto, London, 1970.

Journals and Other Documents on the Life and Voyages of Christopher Columbus. Translated and Edited by Samuel Eliot Morison. Illustrated by Lima De Freitas. 1963.

The Grand Design by Paolo Emilio Taviani. Orbis Publishing Limited. 1985.

Bartholomew de Las Casas, his Life, Apostolate, and Writings by Francis Augustus MacNutt. Cleveland, U.S.A. The Arthur H. Clark Company, 1909.

The Enemies of Christopher Columbus by Thomas A. Bowden. Answers to Critical Questions About the Spread of Western Civilization. Revised Edition. The Paper Tiger, Inc. NY. 2007.

To contact the author, send an e-mail or message to:

officialchristophercolumbus@gmail.com

www.officialchristophercolumbus.com

Made in the USA
Middletown, DE
05 May 2024

53891377R00139